D0979453

TOWARD

the

SETTING SUN

Pioneer Girls Traveling the Overland Trails

Mary Barmeyer O'Brien

TOWARD

the

SETTING SUN

Pioneer Girls Traveling the Overland Trails

TWODOT
HELENA, MONTANA

A · TWODOT · BOOK

© 1999 Mary Barmeyer O'Brien.

Published by Falcon® Publishing, Inc., Helena, Montana.

Printed in Canada.

2 3 4 5 6 7 8 9 0 TP 04 03 02 01 00

Cover photo: Two students at a frontier school in Oregon's logging country. Courtesy of the Division of Special Collections and University Archives, University of Oregon Library System.

Project Editor: Megan Hiller
Production Editor: Jessica Solberg
Copyeditor: Susan Hindman
Cartographer: Tony Moore
Page Compositor: Dana Kim-Wincapaw
Book design by Falcon Publishing, Inc.
Cover design by Jeff Wincapaw

All rights reserved, including the right to reproduce this book or parts thereof in any form, except for inclusion of brief quotations in a review.

Visit our website at www.Falcon.com.

Library of Congress Cataloging-in-Publication Data

O'Brien, Mary Barmeyer.
     Toward the setting sun : pioneer girls traveling the overland
trails / Mary Barmeyer O'Brien.
        p.   cm.
     Includes bibliographical references and index.
     ISBN 1-56044-841-5 (pbk.)
        1. Pioneer children—West (U.S.) Biography.   2. Girls—West (U.S.)
Biography.   3. Overland journeys to the Pacific.   4. Frontier and
pioneer life—West (U.S.)   5. Trails—West (U.S.)—History—19th
century.   6. West (U.S.) Biography.   I. Title.
F593.0285 1999
917.8'042—dc21   99-34695
                                                                         CIP

Falcon® Publishing, Inc.
P. O. Box 1718, Helena, MT 59624

This book is dedicated with love to my husband, Dan, with thanks for his unending encouragement and steady support, and to our children, Jennifer, Kevin, and Katie, who are blazing their own remarkable trails.

CONTENTS

Acknowledgments ix

Introduction xii

Map of Trails xvi

Snowbound in the Sierras:
The Story of Virginia Reed 1

To the Land of Gold and Italian Skies:
The Story of Sallie Hester 13

Wild Roses for Louvina:
The Story of Mary Ellen Todd 21

Heartbreak and Hope on the Applegate Trail:
The Story of Lucy Ann Henderson 33

And in My Heart the Meadow Lark Still Gaily,
Sweetly Sings:
The Story of Laura Elizabeth Ingalls 41

A Child Bride:
The Story of Mary Perry 51

Orphaned on the Oregon Trail:
The Story of Catherine Sager 57

One Stew Kettle to Her Name:
The Story of Martha Ann Morrison 67

Trouble on the Gila Trail:
The Stories of Susan Thompson and
Olive Oatman 75

Bibliography 85

Index 90

About the Author.. 94

ACKNOWLEDGMENTS

I'd like to express my heartfelt appreciation and thanks to those who have helped see *Toward the Setting Sun* to completion, including:

- The ten courageous and invincible girls whose stories are told on these pages, for recording their remarkable wagon journeys and for leaving us their spirited legacies;

- My editor, Megan Hiller, and the staff at Falcon Publishing, for their exceptional work and continual support;

- My family and friends, one and all, for their interest, love, and encouragement;

- Fellow writers Maggie Plummer, Mac Swan, and our daughter Jennifer O'Brien for patiently critiquing my work;

- The staff at Polson City Library for their expert help in carrying out my research, especially Marilyn Trosper, who encouraged and assisted me with her interest and expertise, and Rita Bell for her patience in locating and ordering interlibrary loan materials for me;

- The many others along the way who also aided with my research, including:

  - Bob Clark of the Montana Historical Society and Robert Schuler of the Tacoma Public Library for locating the work of Mary Perry Frost;

- Peter J. Blodgett and Brooke M. Black of California's Huntington Library for their help in obtaining the journals of Catherine Sager Pringle and Susan Thompson Lewis;
- John Mead of the Oregon Historical Society Library for his help in finding the writings of Lucy Henderson Deady and of John Minto;
- Bonnie Hardwick and Peter Hanff of the University of California's Bancroft Library for their assistance in procuring the manuscript of Martha Ann Morrison Minto;
- Stephen Charter, reference archivist, and Carol Singer, reference librarian, at Ohio's Bowling Green State University for making Olive Ann Oatman's personal narrative available to me;
- The accommodating staff at each of the following:
  - The Spokane, Washington, Public Library;
  - The Salem, Oregon, Public Library;
  - The Detroit, Michigan, Public Library;
  - The Laura Ingalls Wilder Memorial Society, Inc., in De Smet, South Dakota;
  - The Laura Ingalls Wilder/Rose Wilder Lane Home and Museum in Mansfield, Missouri;
  - The Chambers of Commerce in Independence, Kansas, and Pepin, Wisconsin.

Special Note: The letters, diaries, oral histories, narratives, and books recorded or written by the girls in this volume (as children or later as adults) are cited in the bibliographies at the end of the book. I have occasionally used their own words to help tell their stories. All excerpts are presented as closely to the original as possible, including unusual spellings, punctuation, and grammar.

ACKNOWLEDGMENTS

I am particularly grateful to those who gave permission to reprint quotes from these original diaries or memoirs, especially:

- The Huntington Library, San Marino, California, for permission to quote from the journal of Catherine Sager Pringle (FAC 600);

- The Bancroft Library, University of California, Berkeley, for permission to quote from the original manuscript, *Female Pioneering in Oregon*, a dictation of Martha Ann Morrison Minto taken by H. H. Bancroft, 1878, (P-A 51);

- The Arthur H. Clark Company, for permission to reprint quotations from the diary of Sallie Hester.

INTRODUCTION

With battered covered wagons as their homes, pioneer children of the 1840s to 1860s joined their parents in the great migration to the beckoning American frontier. Week after week, they trudged toward the setting sun, helping their families cross the huge, rugged landscapes of the West.

Blessed with the exuberance of youth, young people at first viewed their journeys as tremendous adventures. Crossing the continent seemed like an all-summer picnic, a "frolic," as more than one young person described it. As the wagons rumbled away from their homelands, they held foot races, played hide-and-seek by moonlight, and picked bouquets of fragrant wildflowers. When the companies stopped for a time, they hung swings from overhanging tree boughs and took turns sailing into the blue summer skies.

But overland travel was grueling, and the children were desperately needed to help make the undertaking a success—or in many instances, to get their families through alive. Taking a covered wagon from the jump-off points along the Missouri River to Oregon, California, or any other far-off destination was dangerous, daunting, and sometimes impossible. In addition to the trials of life in the wilderness, there were the challenges of crossing roaring streams and steep rocky slopes and of outlasting scorching deserts and pushing through forests tangled with thick undergrowth. Still, promises of hidden gold or a better life in the open spaces of rich, free farmland drew the overland travelers to the frontier like a magnet.

Traveling the almost impassable trails, families were burdened with unrelenting hard work, forcing them to depend upon their children as they never had before. Herding the loose stock animals—the pioneers' most valuable resource—was a job often given to the older boys, who spent their days with the horses and cattle in the choking dust behind the wagons. Girls were pressed into service to keep their many younger brothers and sisters safe from the countless dangers along the trail, to help with the never-ending cooking, and to set up and strike camp. Before long, pioneer children were gathering buffalo chips for campfire fuel instead of picking wildflowers, and they were too tired and footsore from tramping behind the oxen or beside the wagons to find running races appealing. Usually they had great responsibility, despite their young age. "I have driven many a mile, child as I was," remembered Martha Ann Morrison, who was twelve when she helped take her family's wagons west in 1844.

Of course, not every moment was filled with work and strain. Young people found joy in picking ripe berries along the mountain trails, or sipping bubbly, sweetened water from Idaho's Soda Springs. They found peace in rocking their newborn brothers or sisters, and they savored the smell of antelope stew bubbling over a campfire. Some loved to lope across the plains on horseback; others enjoyed carving their names in soft stone landmarks along the way. They formed warm friendships, waded in clear streams, or threw snowballs if they happened upon a patch of old snow.

Unfortunately, nearly every family experienced some sort of trauma during the trip. The death of a parent, sibling, or friend was common, and so were diseases like typhoid and cholera. Fierce lightning storms, terrifying river crossings, and wagon rollovers all helped shape the characters of the young travelers. Some endured hunger to the brink of starvation. Others survived snake bites or broken bones. Cold rain and snow soaked their bedding and clothes as they toiled their way to the promised land. Always, their lives hung in balance—and many of them, wise beyond their years, knew it.

Adversities built character and strength in these soon-to-be adults. Girls, especially, had to summon strength far beyond the usual submissiveness expected of them. Susan Thompson, for example, led her family through a southwestern desert while her father lay delirious from illness in the wagon and her mother was confined with a newborn baby. Catherine Sager watched five family members die— and later, her adopted parents as well—but still managed to go on and live a productive life on the frontier. Olive Oatman, who was taken captive by Apaches, relied on her devout faith in God to survive her experiences. And Virginia Reed, who went to the edge of death and back snowbound with her family in the high Sierra Nevadas, learned the value of life itself.

Girls of the era were expected to be ladylike, with modest manners and gentle personalities. They were to speak in low voices and wear sunbonnets to protect their complexions. On the westward trails, however, these same girls had to develop physical strength and stamina, courage, and inner fortitude. To survive the toil and heartache of their journeys, many were forced to set aside some of their ideas about femininity, and of necessity, herd cattle and drive wagons, build cook fires, and haul belongings up the steepest slopes. Barefoot and suntanned, they worked constantly to help their families survive one of the most difficult migrations of all time.

Each of the resilient girls and young women on the following pages left behind a record of her experiences on the westward trails. Some wrote diaries or later memoirs of their remarkable trips, recording events that shaped their lives in the new land. Others told their oral histories in well-remembered detail. A few sent poignant letters to friends and family back home, telling of their struggles. Laura Ingalls Wilder wrote a series of beloved children's books about her pioneer life. No matter how the overland experiences were recorded, each preserved a piece of history unique to her own time, place, and circumstance.

There are places in the West where the deep, gouged wagon tracks of these intrepid travelers are visible today, a century and a half later. Occasionally we can see their tumble-down log cabins, long since abandoned but rich with history. Their stories, too, are with us still— unforgettable legacies that live on despite the passage of years.

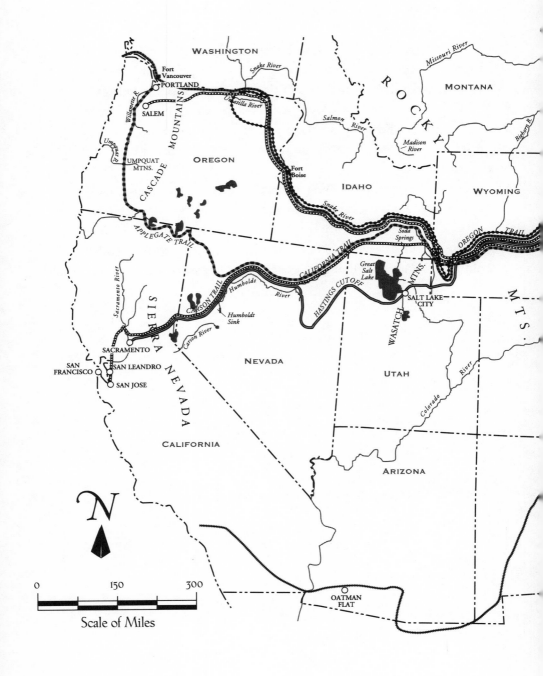

ROCKY

WASHINGTON

MONTANA

Missouri River

Fort Vancouver

Snake River

PORTLAND

Willamette R.

SALEM

Salmon River

Umpqua R.

UMPQUAT MTNS.

OREGON

Umatilla River

Fort Boise

IDAHO

Madison River

Bighorn R.

CASCADE MOUNTAINS

WYOMING

Snake River

APPLEGATE TRAIL

Soda Springs

OREGON TRAIL

SIERRA NEVADA

CARSON TRAIL

CALIFORNIA TRAIL

Humboldt River

Great Salt Lake

HASTINGS CUTOFF

WASATCH MTNS.

Sacramento River

Humboldt Sink

Carson River

NEVADA

SALT LAKE CITY

MTS.

SACRAMENTO

SAN FRANCISCO

SAN LEANDRO

SAN JOSE

UTAH

Colorado River

CALIFORNIA

ARIZONA

N

0   150   300

Scale of Miles

OATMAN FLAT

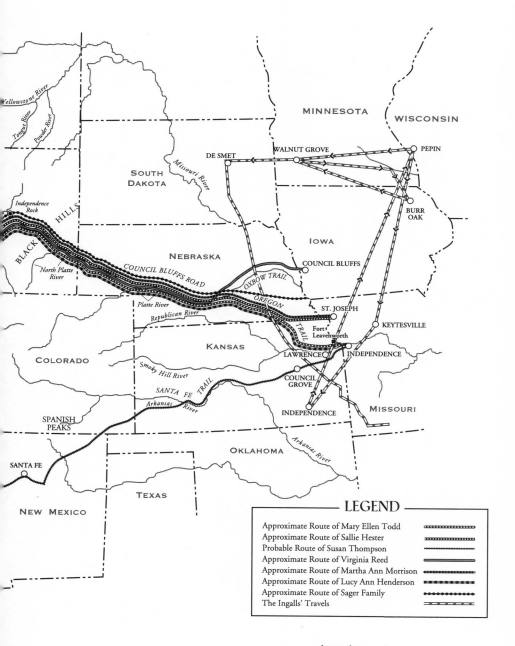

YELLOWSTONE RIVER
Tongue River
Powder River

MINNESOTA
WISCONSIN

SOUTH DAKOTA
Missouri River

DE SMET
WALNUT GROVE
PEPIN

BURR OAK

Independence Rock
BLACK HILLS

COUNCIL BLUFFS ROAD
North Platte River
OXBOW TRAIL
OREGON TRAIL

IOWA

COUNCIL BLUFFS

NEBRASKA

Platte River
Republican River

ST. JOSEPH
Fort Leavenworth
KEYTESVILLE

COLORADO

KANSAS
Smoky Hill River
SANTA FE TRAIL
Arkansas River

LAWRENCE
INDEPENDENCE

COUNCIL GROVE

SPANISH PEAKS

INDEPENDENCE
MISSOURI

Arkansas River

OKLAHOMA

SANTA FE

NEW MEXICO

TEXAS

LEGEND

Approximate Route of Mary Ellen Todd	··············
Approximate Route of Sallie Hester	··············
Probable Route of Susan Thompson	————————
Approximate Route of Virginia Reed	————————
Approximate Route of Martha Ann Morrison	●●●●●●●●●●
Approximate Route of Lucy Ann Henderson	■■■■■■■■■
Approximate Route of Sager Family	●●●●●●●●●
The Ingalls' Travels	═══════

the TRAILS

SNOWBOUND IN THE SIERRAS
The Story of Virginia Reed

Thirteen-year-old Virginia Reed sat huddled in the corner of the cold, damp shack. Although she was desperately hungry, she wondered how she could stand to swallow the small, cold, glue-like piece of congealed broth that was her day's only meal. But there was nothing else to eat. The fourteen others stranded with her in the tiny snow-buried shelter were sharing the small gelatinous mass that her mother had made by boiling ox hides. Virginia knew she needed to eat hers to keep up her failing strength.

Outside, the wind shrieked through the icy pines, but Virginia could hardly hear it. Deep snow had buried the makeshift hut. Winter was harsh in the high Sierra Nevadas, and the stalled travelers of the Donner party knew their lives were in danger.

Virginia thought back to the long covered wagon journey that had brought them from Springfield, Illinois, almost to California. At the beginning of the trip in April 1846, her family had set out comfortably in their three custom-made, well-stocked wagons which were driven by hired drivers. The biggest, a "pioneer palace car" ordered especially by Virginia's stepfather, James Frazier Reed, stood two stories high. Stairs led up the side to a sitting room, which was heated by a small stove. A mirror hung on the wall. Women from the wagon train sometimes gathered there to mend clothes or knit while they chatted with Virginia's mother, Margaret Reed. There, too, was where the Reed's hired girl, Eliza, tended the family's younger children, Patty, James, and Thomas. The other two wagons were filled with provisions and supplies for their new home in California.

The wagon train was made up of several families and single men, and was led by George Donner, an older, well-respected captain. Jumping off from Independence, Missouri, the party traveled easily across the vast green plains of what are now Kansas and Nebraska and along the gentle muddy waters of the Platte River into Wyoming. There was plenty of fresh game to eat, and water and lush grass for the working oxen (the Reeds needed twenty at a time to pull their wagons), horses, milk cows, and Virginia's pony, Billy. During those warm, sunny days, there was no hint of the disaster ahead that would turn the trip into one of the most terrible ordeals ever experienced along the westward trails.

Soon after the Donner party reached the Continental Divide in mid-July, a horseback rider met them with a letter from Lansford W. Hastings, the author of a guidebook about wagon routes to the West. The letter advised all California-bound wagon parties to take a new, shorter cutoff that led south of the Great Salt Lake in today's state of Utah. Hastings promised he would wait for the travelers at Fort Bridger to guide them along this new route, which would save them three hundred to four hundred miles.

When the group reached Fort Bridger, however, the season was late and Hastings had already left with an earlier party of emigrants. Little did the Donner party know that a letter awaited them at the fort that warned them not to take the dangerous cutoff. The letter was never given to them. Hastings' tracks were plainly visible in the deep dust, so on July 31, some of the travelers in the Donner wagon

VIRGINIA REED MURPHY
THE BANCROFT LIBRARY, UNIVERSITY OF CALIFORNIA BERKELEY

train, including Virginia and her family and a few others who joined them, followed them into the dry lands of Utah.

The trip became more and more difficult. Although the emigrants soon knew that taking the cutoff had been a mistake, it was too late to turn back. They toiled over the rough terrain, forced at one point to cut a road through the heavily wooded wilderness. It was "exhausting, backbreaking work," Virginia wrote later, and the wagons made excruciatingly slow progress; it took six days to cover only thirteen miles. Meanwhile, more emigrants caught up with them and joined the train, well aware that the summer days were passing quickly.

When the Donner party finally reached the huge, arid desert country west of the Great Salt Lake, they found travel nearly impossible, but pressed on. The oxen were worn to skeletons, and the travelers were bone-weary and discouraged. Tempers were short. The days that followed were extremely dry and hot, but the nights were miserably cold. Virginia and her sister and brothers shivered under their thin blankets until Mr. Reed "placed all five of our dogs around us" for warmth. Worst of all, their water ran out. The children were begging for a drink, so Mr. Reed left his family and went ahead to search for a spring or river. Disaster struck while he was gone. The family's cattle—all but one cow and one ox—bolted ahead to find water and could not be found, despite several days of weary searching. The Reeds had to abandon two of their three wagons, including their "palace car," and cache their precious belongings. Then, hitching borrowed oxen with their remaining animals, they struggled on with their one small wagon and few provisions, trudging across the endless sand in order to spare the tired animals their weight in the wagon. Later, Virginia wrote to her cousin: "Hastings said it was 40 but i think it was 80 miles." In the meantime, food ran low, and two volunteers were sent ahead to Sutter's Fort (near present-day Sacramento) to get provisions.

Only with extreme determination did the party get through the desert country. But soon after they reached the Humboldt River in today's Nevada, Virginia's stepfather killed another man in a dispute. Although historians believe he may have acted in self-defense, Virginia must have turned cold when the other travelers talked about lynching him. Finally, though, he was simply banished from the wagon train with little but his horse. When darkness fell that sad night, Virginia and one of the family's trusted hired men slipped ahead in the darkness to smuggle him his pistol, his rifle, and some food for the lonely journey to California, where he hoped to reunite with his family. "I cried so hard that I barely had strength to walk," Virginia wrote later. In the morning, she and her mother and the younger children traveled on without him. Before long they were forced to abandon the last heavy wagon and store a few belongings in another family's wagon.

Pushing on, the family watched for any sign of Mr. Reed. Occasionally they found a note from him stuck in a bush, or saw ashes from his fire. Finally, when the volunteers returned from Sutter's Fort with provisions, they reported he had safely reached the settlements.

The trail had led the wagon train across the present state of Nevada. Ahead lay California—on the far side of the high peaks of the Sierra Nevadas, which rose like an impassable wall before them. It was late October and the summits were covered with fresh snow. The emigrants, surprised at encountering winter so near to the warm lands of California, knew they couldn't get the wagons over the pass if the weather got worse.

There was no choice but to try. Up they climbed toward the elusive pass on a steep, rocky trail that required all their remaining strength. The party stretched out, with some hurrying ahead and others following slowly making necessary wagon repairs and resting their animals. Finally, on the cold evening of November 3, 1846, the Reeds and several other families came within three miles of the summit. When the wagons got bogged down in the snow, they abandoned them, tied provisions onto oxen, and made a second attempt. It was unsuccessful. Deathly cold and tired, they decided to camp for the night and cross the demanding pass in the morning.

As darkness fell, the temperature dropped, and the snowflakes began to fall heavily. By morning the drifts were much deeper, and reaching the summit was out of the question. Weak and frightened, the travelers turned back, hoping the snow would melt so they could try the pass again. They floundered back through the drifts, knowing they were in trouble. Near a mountain lake which they called Donner Lake, they found a small shack built by previous travelers, and quickly put up other temporary log shelters in the snow, using their canvas wagon tops or animal hides to cover the roofs. Virginia and her family moved into one. Farther down the trail, the Donners made wigwam-like structures with branches, brush, hides and wagon covers. Wet and cold, they crowded inside. All together, the stranded emigrants numbered about eighty, including forty-one children.

The snow, instead of melting, increased with winter storms. Before long, the emigrants knew they were caught in a terrible trap—and there was no way out until spring. Their provisions were already getting low, almost all their remaining cattle had died, and the snow was so deep that hunting was impossible. Stunned, the party settled in for the terrible weeks ahead.

At first, they hoped a rescue party would find them. Virginia's stepfather had made it to Sutter's Fort. The children knew he would send help when they didn't arrive in California as planned. But as the weather worsened and the days dragged on, it became almost impossible for even the most devoted rescuers to conquer the extreme mountain conditions. Hope diminished along with the meager food supply.

The few remaining cattle were butchered as November turned into December. When snow reached the tops of the shelters, getting firewood became a struggle. Fifteen of the hardiest travelers, weak and hungry though they were, left camp on homemade snowshoes to try to walk to the far-off California settlements for help. They took bits of food to last six days. Those remaining at the mountain camp wondered if they would ever see them again.

Virginia woke up Christmas morning to a breakfast of gluey ox-hide broth. Margaret Reed, despite her own weakness and poor health, was determined that her children would have a small treat that day. She had hoarded a little piece of bacon, a few beans, and some bits of dried apple to cook for dinner. The shelter filled with the delicious aroma of warm food, and Margaret Reed told them that just this once, they could eat all they wanted. Virginia never forgot the joy that simple Christmas meal brought to their otherwise dark and dismal day.

The winter was unrelenting. Storms and blizzards blew in, one after another. Early in January 1847, Margaret Reed, Virginia, and several others made a desperate attempt to escape to safety, but had to return to camp after days of pushing through heavy drifts on frostbitten feet. By then, some of the emigrants had died of starvation. Virginia and her family survived any way they could. Their food was gone, so they were finally forced to boil and eat the hides that covered their shack. When snow blew in, another family, the Breens, allowed the Reeds to crowd into their small cabin with them. Patrick and Margaret Breen, who had seven children, still had a few pieces of beef left, and Virginia later reported that kind Mrs. Breen "saved my life by slipping me a piece of meat now and then. . . ."

7

In the meantime, a few of the snowshoe party, nearly frozen and barely alive, reached the first California settlement. The trip had taken thirty-three days—not the six they had hoped—and eight of the fifteen had died along the way. Delirious from hunger and very near death, the survivors had cannibalized the others' bodies in order to stay alive long enough to get help. In the settlements, relief parties were organized, one of which was headed by Virginia's frantic stepfather, who had already tried and failed at one rescue attempt. The wild ruggedness of the mountains and the tremendous snow depth made rescue nearly impossible.

By mid-January the snow was twelve to fifteen feet deep, and the desperate survivors were eating charred ox bones. The children, who were by then too weak to play on the ice-cold floors of their cramped quarters, stayed in bed to keep from freezing. On stormy days, the women and men had to shovel snow from their makeshift fireplaces and chip pieces of wood from the inside walls of the log shelters to build fires. Day after day the emigrants prayed that God would deliver them from their terrible ordeal. Virginia, watching the Breen's devout Catholic faith, vowed that if God would save her, she, too, would become a Catholic.

As the days dragged on, the families became more miserable. Some were so desperate—and their minds were so dulled from severe hunger—that they, too, turned to cannibalism. Virginia wrote to her cousin that "some . . . was eating from them that Died." A few kept themselves alive this way, but the Reeds were able to survive on ox hides, dog meat, and perhaps even mice that sought shelter in their rough structure.

Then, on the evening of February 19, seven men were spotted struggling toward the camp. A relief party! Joy surged through the starved colony as they said heartfelt prayers of thanks. Exhausted and cold, the men had brought as much food as they could carry, and had cached more food along the escape trail. At last, a true meal! During the next few days, a plan was made to take twenty-three of the Donner party out with the rescuers. Those who were too weak to walk would stay behind and try to wait until another relief party got through.

The Reeds started out with the foot travelers. Margaret, Virginia, and five-year-old Jimmy were able to keep up with the slow progress around Donner Lake and over the steep pass, though they stumbled and fell from weakness. Young Patty and Tommy Reed, though, did not have the strength. Virginia and her mother were devastated when the two were sent back to the shelters to wait. Still, she and the others pushed on. Their feet were frostbitten and bleeding, their scant food was nearly gone, and a terrible discovery was soon made—animals had destroyed the caches of provisions along the trail. Even snow blindness plagued them.

For five days they hauled themselves through the snow. Getting weaker and colder by the moment, they wondered how they could ever cover the rest of the distance. One young man simply stayed behind to die, but the Reeds toiled on, urging little Jimmy ahead with promises of food at the end of the trip.

Just as Virginia felt she couldn't take another step, she looked ahead and saw a sight that etched itself on her memory forever: her stepfather and ten other men laboring toward them! In a few moments she was joyfully stumbling into his strong, welcoming arms. She took him to her mother, who had fallen from weakness and gratitude into the snow, and told him of her little brother and sister back at the shelters. Mr. Reed quickly gave Virginia, Margaret, young Jimmy, and the other feeble travelers food, including some special sweet bread he had baked for them. It was the first bread they had had in months. Then, strengthened with sustenance, the exhausted group prepared to escape from the rugged high country. Mr. Reed and his party set out to rescue his son and daughter and the others still stranded near Donner Lake. A third relief party later arrived to assist.

Virginia and the others slowly descended out of the snow and into the sunny emerald valleys of their long-dreamed-of California. At the first settlement, they were taken in and given emergency care. In the days that followed, they were nursed to health with nourishing food. Reeling from their dreadful winter, they rejoiced in the warm sunshine and were profoundly grateful to bathe, rest, and socialize. Later, after a grueling journey through late-winter blizzards, Mr. Reed triumphantly returned with Tommy and Patty, among others, safely in his care. Inside her clothes, Patty had hidden a small wooden doll that had kept her company at Donner Lake.

Unlike most families in the Donner party, none of the Reeds died from exposure or starvation. The others did not fare so well. Many of the Donners themselves had starved to death, along with about half of the other stranded travelers. Of the forty-one children in the camp, only twenty-six survived. News of their terrible ordeal traveled quickly and served as a warning to other wagon travelers who wished to cross the Sierra Nevadas. Later emigrants became aware of the extreme danger of being caught in the mountains and were careful to cross before the snows settled in. They reported seeing the shelters the Donner party had erected and the trunks of trees cut off for firewood fifteen feet above the ground where the snow level had been those terrible months. That spring, Virginia wrote a letter to her cousin describing their tragic winter and saying: "O Mary I have not wrote you half of the truble we have had but I have Wrote you anuf to let you now that you don't now whattruble is."

When gold was discovered at Sutter's Fort in 1848, Mr. Reed became a successful and wealthy prospector. He and Margaret adopted one of the orphaned Donner children, Mary. Later the family went on to settle near present-day San Jose, where Virginia married at the age of sixteen. She and her husband, John Murphy—who was also wealthy from gold discoveries—lived near her parents, and eventually had nine children, three of whom died as infants.

Although Virginia loved California's warm days and cool nights and was busy with her large family, her thoughts often drifted back to her harrowing experiences in the cold Sierra Nevadas. Later, as an adult, she wrote about her months trapped in that high mountain valley, putting into words the horror she felt, but also recording forever the courage and strength of those who encountered a desperate situation and worked with all their will to survive. Among the things she remembered best were the devout prayers the families shared as they knelt on the cold, hard shelter floor and her vow, which she fulfilled, to join the Catholic faith. She remembered her sister Patty's well-worn little doll, now preserved in a museum, and her mother's kindness and fortitude in providing that never-to-be-forgotten Christmas dinner. And she wrote about her immense gratitude upon reaching California in safety:

> One day, shortly after we arrived . . . I wandered off by myself to a lovely little knoll. I simply stood there in a bed of wildflowers, looking up and down the green valley. The birds were singing in the branches over my head, and the sun was smiling down upon all. I drank it all in for a moment, kissed my hand, then gently blew the kisses from my palm toward heaven in thanksgiving. . . . ▨

To the Land of Gold and Italian Skies

The Story of Sallie Hester

The dark waters of the Missouri River swirled beneath the beached steamboat. Thirteen-year-old* Sallie Hester peered over the railing. Aground on another sandbar! It seemed as if this slow, balky boat would never reach St. Joseph, Missouri, the jumping-off place for her family's covered wagon journey to California in 1849. Already they had been traveling for more than three weeks, first by carriage, and then by boat down the Ohio River and up the Missouri.

So far, the trip had been a mixture of adventure and misfortune. Every few days, Sallie recorded the events in a diary she kept, which described her family's overland journey. Leaving schoolmates and relatives behind in Bloomington, Indiana, had been heartbreaking, and bad roads—rough enough to tip over their carriage—made the long trip to the steamboat seem endless. But Sallie was thrilled by

---

*Although Sallie's diary is subtitled "The Adventures of Sallie Hester, Aged Twelve, in a Trip Overland in 1849," she may actually have been thirteen on her journey west. Historians believe she was born in October 1835.

big cities like St. Louis and Jefferson City, and by her first glimpse of boats and a river.

This time the sandbar had stopped them only ten miles from St. Joseph, where the Hesters were to find their covered wagons waiting, so they disembarked with their carriage and finished the trip overland. Sallie was astonished at the large number of people heading west in wagons, which she called a "vast army on wheels." She and her younger sister, Lottie, watched the hustle and bustle of the busy city with interest. Their mother, Martha, was ill and reluctant to undertake the journey ahead, but their father, successful lawyer Craven P. Hester, wanted to go west. Sallie's brothers, William and John, accompanied them.

The Hesters' canvas-covered wagons and their trusty carriage were carefully stocked with plenty of supplies and ferried across the river. It was early May 1849, and the great gold rush to California had begun. The Hesters, however, were going west in search of better health, not wealth. Wagon train after wagon train set out over the windswept plains, bound for fresh opportunity. As far as the eye could see, there were only waves of prairie grass and jumbles of bright wildflowers.

Native American tribes were becoming increasingly alarmed by the newcomers flooding their ancient lands, and some were attempting to stop the boundless flow of emigrants. The Hesters' train of fifty wagons passed through Pawnee country, an area considered dangerous. At night, the party pulled the heavy wagons into a circle, securing the cattle inside and pitching tents outside. Men stood guard. Sallie and her family slept in the wagons, with their hired drivers nearby.

Surrounded by those she loved and trusted, Sallie snuggled next to her sister in their warm feather bed. Coyotes sang, and the oxen and milk cows chewed their cud. Thousands of stars sparkled in the clear black sky. The smell of campfire smoke mingled with the scents of trampled grass, oxen, and sometimes the dampness of a nearby river. Sallie knew that the trip ahead held jagged mountains she had never seen, wildly tumbling streams that must be crossed, and long sunbaked deserts to endure. Perhaps she wondered what lay ahead for her family and if they would reach California without mishap.

Sallie and Lottie would arise before dawn, as wagon travelers often did, wash their faces in ice-cold river water, and brush and braid their hair before helping their mother with breakfast. First, the hot campfire coals had to be rekindled with sticks or dried buffalo chips. Soon the fragrance of hot coffee would fill the air, followed by the mouth-watering smell of bacon or ham frying, or dried fruit being stewed. The family would eat bread or biscuits with hard-packed butter as they sat on camp stools around their portable table. They used tin dishes and "cheap knives and forks," since their good ones were packed away in the wagon. A sheet iron cooking stove, by then sooty and well used, helped Sallie and her mother prepare the food they needed later for a cold lunch on the trail.

By May 24, about three weeks after they had crossed the Missouri, the family reached the adobe-walled Fort Kearney on the Oregon–California Trail in today's state of Nebraska. A deadly cholera epidemic swept along with them. Sallie wrote in her diary: "The cholera is raging. A great many deaths; graves everywhere." The Hesters somehow stayed healthy, but Mrs. Hester, whose stamina had improved on the trail, longed for her safe home back in Indiana as she saw travelers around her dying of the often fatal, highly contagious disease.

June passed as the wagons wended their way west. The party stopped at Fort Laramie in present-day Wyoming and later crossed the Platte River on a ferry. On July 2, they reached Independence Rock, a landmark where travelers traditionally carved their names. Sallie, too, etched hers in the soft stone.

A few miles on, the party came to Devil's Gate, a narrow canyon where the water was "dashing, splashing and roaring." Sallie, Lottie, their brother John, and another boy climbed to a small, rocky outcrop. Far below, the Sweetwater River foamed and roiled. The four watched in fascination and were gone longer than they intended. Before they knew it, the wagon train had halted and the men went out searching for them. Sallie hinted that she and her companions were scolded when she wrote, "We made all sorts of promises to remain in sight in the future."

The weather was hot. The Hesters and their companions pressed on, crossing the Continental Divide at South Pass. This was such a beautiful, gentle route over the Rocky Mountains that emigrants often had trouble knowing when they had reached the top. But the days following were more difficult. Sallie reported that they "had neither wood nor water for fifty-two miles."

When the wagons would stop for the evening, music filled the camp and echoed from the surrounding mountains. Some of the party's young single men ("jolly, merry fellows," Sallie wrote) had brought their guitars and violins from back home. Under the vast night sky, they sang in strong, clear voices, filling the lonely wilderness with song. Others gathered to listen, most likely around a glowing campfire. Sallie was sorry when in mid-August, these young men decided to leave the slow train to travel at a faster pace, for the evenings seemed empty without their music resounding through the darkness.

As the summer progressed, the fine dust on the trail became nearly intolerable. Men wore "veils tied over their hats," but the grit found its way into every crevice of their clothing. It settled inside the wagons until bedding and supplies were covered, and even got in the food. Still, the party went on through the dry northeast corner of today's Nevada. As they made their way down the long Humboldt River, they knew they still had to cross the difficult Forty Mile Desert ahead

Devil's Gate outcrop where Sallie climbed
for a View of the Sweetwater River
Used by permission, Utah State Historical Society,
all rights reserved. Photo no. 10133

and then the high Sierra Nevadas that separated them from the rich valleys of California.

Sallie must have had a knot in her stomach when she thought about the Forty Mile Desert. It was known as one of the most difficult and dangerous stretches of the trip. Other wagon travelers had nearly perished in its relentless sun. The hot miles often meant death to the travelers' worn livestock. There was no water until the sweltering trail reached the far-off Truckee River near the present-day Nevada-California border. Before starting out, travelers would mound cut grass in their wagons for the oxen to eat during the crossing, and would fill every possible container with water. Still, they often ran out. Sallie's diary tells briefly of their trip through the desolate stretch:

> . . . the mooing of the cattle for water, their exhausted condition, with the cry of 'Another ox down,' . . . and the weary, weary tramp of men and beasts, worn out with heat and famished for water, will never be erased from my memory.

Sallie probably shed tears when they had to leave one of their own faithful oxen behind, lowing in misery under the relentless sun.

Finally, however, they reached the cool waters of the Truckee River. There the exhausted emigrants stopped and allowed their livestock to rest in the high, thick grass with plentiful water nearby. Then they pushed on, crossing the river, not just once, Sallie wrote, but twenty-four times. Sometimes the crossings scared her; one time, as the swift, deep water rushed by, she got so frightened that in a panic she jumped into the water. The current carried her far downstream, and although her diary does not reveal how she was saved, or if she rescued herself, she wrote that she "nearly drowned."

Then came the long climb up the Sierra Nevadas. It was mid-September when the Hesters passed the place where the famous, snowbound Donner party had wintered. Sallie saw two log shelters and treetops cut off at the old snow level. A few miles later, her party finally reached the summit of the great mountain range. Night had fallen as they started carefully down the other side. Since the road was rocky and narrow, Sallie and her family walked, carrying flaming pitch-filled pine knots to light the treacherous way. In the days to follow, they would have to let their wagons down the steep mountain slopes using ropes tied onto strong trees. The descent was so difficult that near an area known as Sleepy Hollow, the Hesters had to abandon one of their wagons.

By then they were in California. So far, it was hardly the "land of gold and Italian skies," as Sallie had once called it. Only thirteen of the original fifty wagons remained. In the scattered settlements, prices were exorbitant, and the weather was cold and rainy. On October 10, 1849, weary but grateful to be near their journey's end, the Hesters stopped in the small village of Fremont to spend the winter. There they had a two-room clapboard cabin built for them, and pitched their traveling tent out back to serve as a storage place. Mr. Hester went to Sacramento to buy supplies for the long, wet season ahead.

On Christmas Day, Sallie wrote that her mother was homesick and unhappy. Then in mid-January, the nearby river flooded its banks and swamped the town of Fremont. Sallie wrote: "Nearly everybody is up to their knees in mud and water. . . . It's horrible. Wish I was back in Indiana. Snakes are plenty. They come down the river, crawl under our beds and everywhere."

But circumstances gradually improved. Soon Sallie was writing about the letters she received from fondly remembered schoolmates back home, and of new friends she was making in California. They invited her to social events, including a candy pull, where she met several "nice young men." She commented that "I am too young for beaux, but the young men don't seem to think so." In the meantime,

Mr. Hester traveled to beautiful, warm San Jose and decided to move the family there. The following spring, in May 1850, they made the final leg of their journey. Sallie started school, and she met Margaret Reed of the Donner party who invited her to come practice on their piano. Sallie wrote with enthusiasm that she went "every day."

Her teenage years and young adulthood were lived out in sunny San Jose, where her father was a judge for many years. On October 5, 1871, she married James K. Maddock and they moved to Eureka, Nevada. There her diary ends.

Gifted with unusually fine literacy for a child of her time, Sallie Hester added her story to the literature of the westward movement. As she dabbled her toes in the refreshing waters of the Truckee or the Sweetwater—or listened to the strains of guitars echoing off the craggy Rocky Mountains—she diligently wrote down each day's events. One hundred and fifty years later, her story shines across the years, carving a niche in history for this bright young girl of the California Gold Rush. ▦

WILD ROSES FOR LOUVINA
The Story of Mary Ellen Todd

Mary Ellen Todd watched her father emerge from the family tent where her little sister, Louvina, lay stricken with cholera. He spoke softly to his wife, who was in the nearby covered wagon, asking her to find their small looking glass. The request troubled nine-year-old Mary Ellen. She knew that Louvina lay deathly still, never moving or responding. Why did their father, who had nursed the little girl devotedly for those long, dreadful days, need a mirror?

When she quietly asked, Mary Ellen's stepmother told her the truth. No one could tell if Louvina was still alive. Her breathing had become so shallow her father could no longer hear it, and he couldn't see her thin chest rise and fall. The mirror might help him answer the terrible question. If slight condensation formed when he placed it at her mouth, he would know Louvina was breathing. Mary Ellen's heart ached. Tears formed in her eyes as she wandered a little way from the wagon. Louvina couldn't die. Whatever would she do without her beloved companion and playmate? Would her parents ever lose the sad, haggard look that had settled onto their faces here on the enormous plains along the Oregon–California Trail? The huge

21

dome of sky dwarfed the big wagon and their tent as the family waited and prayed fervently that Louvina would recover.

Mary Ellen walked down to the river. Ahead she saw something small and pink. Wild roses were blooming along the sandy banks of the Platte River. Avoiding the needle-sharp thorns, she picked a bouquet of the lovely flowers, whose fragrance made her forget her sadness for a moment. Returning to camp, she heard her tired father murmuring the Twenty-third Psalm inside the tent, so she put the flowers in an old pickle jar and set them outside the canvas door flap. A few moments later, Mr. Todd came to the opening looking relieved. Louvina was breathing, he reported, and he thought she might be a tiny bit better. He took the roses inside while Mary Ellen hurried to the campfire to heat some nourishing milk for her father to drip into Louvina's mouth.

The next morning, Mary Ellen could hear her father singing hymns. Louvina was indeed better! She had even opened her eyes and noticed the beautiful wild roses. Almost immediately, the heaviness lifted from Mary Ellen's heart. She ran to the river to gather a fresh bouquet. Louvina would need rest and tender care, but Mary Ellen knew she would recover from the awful cholera that had nearly claimed her life. After the tent was disinfected and the bedclothes boiled, the family could roll on toward Oregon again. Perhaps, just perhaps, her offering of wild roses had helped fan the spark of life that saved Louvina. That day Mary Ellen, too, was able to sing, entertaining the family's toddler, Cynthia, with her songs.

When Abbot and Angelina Todd and their family left their home in Arkansas in April 1852, they anticipated hardship on the trail. But the stories that made their way back from Oregon Territory were mostly about fertile valleys, a pleasant climate, and free land, and not as much about cholera and other hazards of the overland journey. The family had prepared with care. Abbot Todd had acquired a team

CROSSING A BRIDGE ON THE WAY WEST
THE DENVER PUBLIC LIBRARY, WESTERN HISTORY COLLECTION

of eight strong oxen and other stock. Their large, red-wheeled wagon was loaded with sugar, flour, corn meal, hams, dried fruit, lard, and additional provisions. Tied onto the back were two chairs he had made, along with the ever-important water bucket. A brass kettle and frying pan hung nearby. Readily accessible were dishes, cookware, and extra clothing for the family of five and the teenaged neighbor boy—John Ragsdale—who accompanied them. There was a tar bucket to use when the wheels needed greasing, a gun for hunting, and medicine, as well as a padded box to serve as a crib for little Cynthia. Everything was packed and repacked until it fit, since nothing could be left behind.

The family waved a tearful last good-bye to their Arkansas friends and relatives and set out for Independence, Missouri, a jumping-off point for Oregon travelers. There were farmhouses along the way, offering shelter from the frequent spring storms. On that first leg of their journey, the Todds learned how to pack the crowded wagon more efficiently, how to churn cream into butter by simply hanging it in a covered bucket under the jostling wagon all day, and how to make good sourdough bread with only a campfire for cooking. Before long, they had reached Independence, where they joined a party of about a hundred westward-bound wagons. A captain and other officers were elected, and then the train was ready to cross the Missouri River and set off for the frontier.

As they journeyed the first few hundred miles, one by one the wagons turned around and returned home. Cholera was raging along the Platte River on the Oregon–California Trail, and the emigrants were afraid of the deadly disease, which they knew was extremely contagious. Others turned back, fearful of crossing the mighty, rushing streams that roared across their trail. Before long, only the Todds and three other families remained. They were determined to persevere with their plans to reach Oregon, realizing that their odyssey had barely begun.

In an oral history recorded later by her daughter, Mary Ellen recalled reaching the wide, swift Kaw River in today's northern Kansas. With trepidation, they prepared to cross. The wagon beds were emptied, taken off, and sealed with tar and rosin so they could be used as boats. Then they were launched into the raging water. Loaded with the family's belongings, they were forced across the dangerous current using ropes and chains. Several perilous trips had to be made to ferry across the animals, supplies, wagon parts, and especially the children. When it was her turn to cross, Mary Ellen shut her eyes so she wouldn't see the dark, swirling water. It was a long, tiring day, but finally the four families completed their passage safely.

The Todds held fast to their ties to civilization. As they left Kansas and headed out onto the Nebraska plains, Mary Ellen memorized Bible lessons, and Louvina learned to read simple words. They decorated their wagon with garlands of wildflowers. Angelina Todd urged her girls to wear sunbonnets to protect their complexions, and she gave them special lotion to put on their hands and faces to keep their skin soft despite the harsh sun, wind, and dust. The girls wove fresh flower wreaths for little Cynthia to wear in her hair. If they rode horseback, they sat sidesaddle as was customary for women. Mary Ellen recalled that:

Mother was always reminding Louvina and me to be ladies, but sometimes it seemed to me that the requirements were too rigid, for I also liked to run, jump and climb, yet I did try to keep from talking and laughing loudly; also I did not often interrupt when others, especially elderly people, were talking. Yes, we heard a great deal about politeness.

The Todds were an especially loving family who spoke cordially to one another and helped each other with daily tasks. Angelina Todd, whom Mary Ellen remembered as beautiful and always busy, even made a pair of cotton-padded canvas booties for the family dog, Rover, when his paws became sore and trail-worn. At first, the dog tried to get them off, but soon got used to wearing them, and his raw feet recovered nicely. The family treated its oxen kindly, too, cushioning their yokes and taking extra time to let them rest and graze. This slowed the group's pace until two of the remaining four families went on ahead, impatient with the delays. The Todds and their friends, the Grants, traveled on alone.

As they moved slowly across the plains, Abbot Todd made a point of stopping to help others in trouble, offering words of encouragement, medicine, or supplies to those in need. The family heard stories of conflicts with the Native American tribes of the plains, but Abbot calmed the children's fears by helping them understand the problems. He suggested that the white settlers were crowding the Indians out by killing the buffalo and taking over the land that rightfully belonged to them, and that whites "had not always treated the Indians right." These unusual views were contrary to the prevailing opinions of the day, and Mary Ellen remembered that they helped her feel "more kindly."

After Louvina's bout with cholera, the two families entered present-day Wyoming. There the roads became more rocky and mountains began to appear. Mary Ellen remembered one terrible downpour of rain and hail, with lightning that struck one of their companions' iron-rimmed wagon wheels. Thunder cracked, and wind roared about them, threatening to upset the wagon. The oxen had to be held by their horns to prevent them from bolting into the wilderness. When the storm was over, two feet of water surrounded the wagons.

By the time the two families worked their way past old Fort Laramie and the Sweetwater and Green Rivers, the dangers of the trail had become more frequent. At one point, Mr. Grant got lost on a hunting side trip, and nearly perished from exhaustion and thirst before he was rescued. On another occasion, a band of Shoshones surrounded their wagons, and Mary Ellen remembered the ensuing scuffle. Outnumbered, the two families feared the worst, but just then a party of hunters from a nearby wagon train appeared over a hill. The Shoshone scattered. Shaken, the Todds and Grants gratefully joined the train temporarily, reaching Fort Hall in present-day Idaho safely.

At Fort Hall, the family decided to join a different, smaller Oregon-bound wagon train, since it meant less structured traveling for Angelina Todd, who was expecting a baby soon. They struck out through dusty sagebrush country along the cliffs high above the Snake River. Instead of firewood or buffalo chips, the families now burned pieces of sagebrush, which gave off an objectionable odor. By then it was mid-August, and the travelers were worried about getting snowbound in the Blue and Cascade Mountains ahead. They knew they "must move along at any cost. . . ," so when a few members of the party showed symptoms of what was called "mountain fever," they continued along the trail. To add to the problems, the terrain became more rocky, and the oxen began giving out. In order to lighten the wagons, the party left behind some of their treasured furniture, but the strain was taking its toll on both the emigrants and their animals.

Suddenly, sickness once again struck the Todds. It was Mary Ellen who first came down with mountain fever, which she later thought to be Rocky Mountain spotted fever, a serious illness caused by tick bite. As she lay in the wagon, jouncing along the stony road, she recalled "How I did want to stop and rest!" Typical of the disease, delirium overtook her. Her stepmother and father nursed her carefully

27

as they hurried on—wishing they could stop to rest and allow her to recuperate, but desperate to cross the mountains before winter set in. Several days passed. Mary Ellen was in a haze, deliriously singing to herself in the wagon. Then, miraculously, as they got closer to Fort Boise, she began to improve. The worst was over—or so they thought.

Just ahead lay the difficult Blue Mountains, but by then the Todds were seasoned travelers. The grades were steep and the trail rocky and difficult. With perseverance, the party slowly made it to the top and down the other side ahead of the snow, using chains to lock the wagons' wheels down the steepest slopes. It was September, and one of the things Mary Ellen remembered most was how she craved fresh vegetables. "I was getting so hungry for green things that I chewed sticks and twigs," she said. She also recalled the area's forests of beautiful evergreen trees—something they had not yet encountered on the journey.

Finally, they neared the Columbia River, the last leg of their transcontinental journey. There, two events occurred that Mary Ellen would remember all her life. First, when the children awoke one morning, they found their stepmother had given birth to a baby boy, whom the family named Elijah. Cuddled against her in the wagon, the infant instantly captured Mary Ellen's heart. They stopped for one precious day, while Abbot Todd did the cooking and washing, and took little Cynthia with him wherever he went. The next morning they set out again.

As they crept along, Mary Ellen noticed her father was not his usual energetic, cheerful self. He "dragged around, making fires and seeing to mother . . . and also driving his team," she related. Before long, it was obvious he had mountain fever. With his typical patience and fortitude, Abbot Todd fought the disease as he struggled to care for those around him, but soon he was so sick he had to retreat to the wagon, where he lay in misery.

Mary Ellen recalled how distressing it was to the children to see their strong, capable father "muttering and groaning with fever." His appetite failed and he was very weak. Mary Ellen almost certainly was afraid her beloved father would die of the debilitating disease, as several of their fellow travelers had. Even if he lived, how would they reach their destination before snowfall if their father was too sick to move the wagon, and their stepmother was still in bed with her newborn? It was surely one of the most dreadful times of the journey, and Abbot Todd himself must have despaired about what would become of them.

Fortunately, John Ragsdale, the neighbor boy who had accompanied the family, was able to take care of the animals, set up the sleeping tent, and make the meals. The children tried to care for their father in the same careful and gentle way he had cared for them, encouraged that he could at least drink tea—and that he wasn't delirious. He could talk with them and instruct them about what to do. After only one day's stop, they moved on down the trail. Slowly, Abbot Todd regained his strength until he could help with the never-ending work. Mary Ellen was thoroughly relieved that her father, who was the recognized strength of the group, was recovering, even if he did look "so weary, and was so quiet." They continued their journey down the wide Columbia River.

Some of their party decided to finish the journey by boat down the Columbia, so the Todds completed their trip to the rich valleys of Oregon alone over the Barlow Road, near Mount Hood. By then it was October, and they knew it was imperative to get through quickly and settle in for the winter. With as much energy as they had left, they tackled the Cascade Mountains. Here was the last big obstacle to their successful journey: the dreaded Laurel Hill, a long, nearly perpendicular descent that the family viewed "in alarm." Abbot Todd hitched a tree to the back of the wagon to help with braking, and attached a rope and chain to the wagon which he wound around a large standing tree at the top of the slope. Even with the brake set at the last notch, the heavy wagon teetered over the edge and hurtled down the mountain, "jamming and shoving" the oxen along as the family watched anxiously from a safe distance. By the time they reached the bottom, the oxen were galloping and the huge, careening wagon looked as if it would surely run them over. The brakes were squealing, as the great iron-clad wheels clattered over the rocks at high speed. Just when disaster seemed certain, the wagon screeched to a halt, still upright. With relief and cheers, the family joined the frightened oxen at the bottom of the hill.

Six months after they started out, the Todds reached Howell's Prairie, not far from Salem, Oregon. They immediately gave thanks for their safe arrival, each saying what had made them most grateful along the hard route. Mary Ellen said she was glad her father hadn't been sick long, and Louvina appreciated the milk their cow gave them along the way. Little Cynthia liked her baby brother best. Angelina Todd was simply glad they had all made it through alive.

Abbot Todd, who later became an ordained minister, rented forty acres and fixed up a small cabin for the family. There they spent their first winter in the new land. Mary Ellen recollected that they celebrated a happy Christmas together by decorating the cabin with evergreens and vines, singing hymns, playing games, and making popcorn.

A few years later, Mary Ellen married John Applegate, a member of the Applegate family so well remembered in Oregon history. Mary Ellen and John eventually moved back along the Oregon Trail to the Snake River area where the Todds had traveled when Mary Ellen was a child. On the border of today's Idaho, they raised stock and founded a home well known to the surrounding settlers for its warm hospitality. The couple had several children.

When their daughter, Adrietta Applegate Hixon, was an elderly woman, she wrote down her mother's trail memories word for word as she clearly recalled them. She noted that Mary Ellen Todd Applegate had a "remarkable memory, and it was her delight to tell these many incidents of her early life." In fact, Mary Ellen had related the stories so well that her daughter "despaired of being able to reproduce her story." While she was writing it, however, the words came alive. It was as if she could almost still hear Mary Ellen's soft voice telling her children and then her grandchildren about her experiences on the overland trail and about her remarkable family of kind and devout pioneers. ▩

HEARTBREAK AND HOPE ON THE APPLEGATE TRAIL

The Story of Lucy Ann Henderson

Eleven-year-old Lucy Henderson wiped her mouth. The bottled medicine she had found swinging in its little bag from the covered wagon's sideboard tasted awful. She and her friend had sneaked a drop just to see. Now her little sister, Lettie, wanted to try it, too. Lucy firmly told her "no" and carefully hung the bag containing the laudanum back on its nail. Then she and her playmate scampered off into the late summer sunshine along the rocky Applegate Trail.

Left alone, little Lettie reached for the bottle herself. She took a big swallow, then another and another, until the opium-based mixture was gone. Feeling sleepy, she went to find her mother, but seeing that she was busy, lay down and fell into a deep slumber. Lettie never awoke. Lucy recalled the terrible incident later in her life when, as an elderly woman, she recorded her reminiscences: "When mother tried to awake her later she couldn't arouse her. Lettie had drunk the whole bottle of laudanum. It was too late to save her life."

The girls' father took the black walnut boards he had brought on their westward journey to use as a table and sadly made them into a coffin. Grieving together, the family buried their little Lettie "by the roadside in the desert."

It was a crushing event for the Hendersons, who were bound for Oregon to join their relatives. They had set out from Missouri in the spring of 1846 along with hundreds of other wagons carrying families west. The travelers were excited and boisterous, the cattle strong, and the food plentiful. Some of the white canvas wagon covers were brightly painted with zealous political slogans urging the United States to fight the British over the jointly occupied Oregon country. "54°40' or Fight!" was the cry of new settlers who flocked to the area wanting full claim to the rich country north to that latitude. But President James Polk decided the border issue in a compromise with the British: the Forty-ninth Parallel would form the upper boundary of the United States. Lucy's family would settle well south of that line.

The Hendersons almost certainly traveled at first on the Oregon–California Trail, which paralleled the shallow Platte River through the prairies of today's Nebraska. Flowers blossomed amid the waving grasses except in places where livestock from earlier wagon trains had grazed them away. Sometimes the westward trail fanned out into many sets of ruts, instead of being a single, well-worn track across the lonesome space. Campsites of previous travelers were visible: traces of cooking fires, heavily trampled foliage, discarded belongings, and even grave markers. Always, up ahead, the wilderness beckoned, calling the emigrants west into its wild beauty. Lucy remembered the confusion the emigrants felt over which trail to take, and the "contradictory reports" and misinformation that circulated about which route was easier or shorter. In the end, they had to rely on their own judgment and hearsay in deciding which of the rough roads was the best choice.

The beginning of the journey passed fairly uneventfully for Robert and Rhoda Henderson and their children, as it did for most emigrants, except for the "violent thunder storms with torrential rains" their wagon party encountered. They filled Lucy with terror. As the fierce spring wind blew, hard rain soaked the family and their belongings, the cattle tried to bolt, and the sleeping tents were blown down. One fellow wagon traveler, J. Quinn Thornton, who followed the same route west and whom Lucy would later know in Oregon, wrote: "The earth itself seemed to tremble beneath the tremendous voice of the thunder. . . . It pealed, crackled, crashed, and bellowed in deafening sounds, that rolled in tumultuous eddies, and awed and hushed the very soul." Lucy may have huddled in a damp wool shawl, terrified that even the two thousand-pound wagon in which she sat would be tipped over by the gale. But the wild winds of the Platte River grasslands blew themselves out, and the Hendersons were able to dry their belongings and move on to Fort Laramie.

After a short stop, they set out over the long, difficult stretch between Fort Laramie and Fort Hall. Lucy's mother was expecting a child soon but the party pushed on, turning south on the California Trail and working its way along the banks of the Humboldt River. At Lassen Meadows in present-day Nevada, a new road, the Applegate Trail, turned off, winding its way into Oregon from below. Lucy reported that her wagon party was the first to take the "Southern Cut-off" as it was called, and they were guided by those who had discovered it, including Jesse Applegate himself. While the wagons crawled over the untamed terrain, some of the men went ahead to make the trail passable. Lucy told of one exhausting two-day desert crossing east of the Cascade Mountains where water was nowhere to be found, and where the cattle and oxen pulling the wagons were nearly frantic from thirst: "We had no grain or hay for the cattle, so

INTERIOR OF AN EMIGRANT WAGON
OREGON HISTORICAL SOCIETY #837, OrHi 55997, INGVARD EIDE

mother baked up a lot of bread to feed them. When we had finally crossed the desert the cattle smelled water, and we couldn't stop them. They ran as hard as they could go, our wagon bouncing along and nearly bouncing us out."

It was there where Lettie Henderson drank the laudanum and died. But three days later, as the desolate family plodded onward without their little girl, another event happened that brought them hope. Lucy's mother gave birth to a baby girl whom they named Olivia. As the brand new infant squalled and batted her fists, perhaps Lucy felt the tight sadness in her chest lift a bit. Later, along the trail, she almost certainly helped hold and care for her baby sister, marveling at her smooth skin and tiny fingers. Perhaps Olivia was the gleam of hope that the weary and discouraged family needed to see them through to Oregon.

By then the days were shorter, the air was beginning to feel crisp, and the party was worried about being caught by the heavy rains and cold snows of autumn. So a few hours after Olivia was born, the wagon train started on its way again, jolting into every hole until the men finally walked beside the wagons trying to "ease the wheels down into the rough places. . . ." Lucy's mother attempted to rest inside with her newborn but found it nearly impossible with the violent jostling and jarring. At one point along the way, the wagons crossed a river on piled-up stones that formed a sort of bridge.

The trail got worse when the fall rains began, and the travelers were still a long way south of their destination: the beautiful, longed-for Willamette Valley. Following the bed of a creek through a steep, rocky canyon, the oxen slipped and fell pulling the heavy wagons—which sometimes tipped onto their sides—over the slippery boulders. In Lucy's reminiscence, she said, "I have never, before or since, seen such rough going." The pioneers discarded everything they could to lighten their loads, even sentimental heirlooms they had lugged hundreds of miles across the plains, but their progress was agonizingly slow. Food had become short. Winter approached as they struggled through dark, dense forests and thick foliage. Finally Lucy's uncle, who was already settled in Oregon, heard of their desperation and came to relieve them with food and horses.

Lucy finished her trip on horseback, clinging to her uncle's back as they crossed the last of the overgrown terrain. Her father stayed behind to see the battered wagon through, and caught up with his family in the Willamette Valley on Christmas Day, 1846. They spent the winter in a one-room cabin with a dirt floor owned by another of Lucy's uncles, somewhere south of the city of Portland. Resourceful Rhoda Henderson filled a big chest with clothing to create a bed for Lucy and her sister, and fed her family boiled wheat and peas until the following spring.

Lucy's father received a donation land claim in the rich green valley and built a log cabin there for his family. Then in the early spring of 1849, at the peak of the gold rush, he left Oregon by ship to seek his fortune in the gold fields of California. The family was poor, and when he returned in the fall, he brought with him "quite a little money." It enabled Lucy to attend a prominent, private school in Oregon City, where she met some of the leaders and influential citizens of the area. There Lucy first saw her future husband, handsome Matthew P. Deady, a schoolteacher, when he came to deliver a letter to her.

The next year, when Lucy was fifteen, she went to school in the settlement of Lafayette. She saw Matthew at church services, and they also "met occasionally at weddings and other social doings." Lucy admired the way he handled a horse and his prowess at swimming. The two were married on June 24, 1852, when Lucy was seventeen. She reported that she wore a pretty, filmy, handmade wedding dress trimmed with silk ribbons, a straw bonnet with streamers, white kid slippers, and gloves.

By then, Matthew had been elected to Oregon Territory's House of Representatives and had resumed an earlier legal career. He was eleven years older than Lucy, and was already well known throughout the area. During their years together, he held prominent positions in the judicial system of the territory and, later, of the new state of Oregon. He was known as Judge Deady, and that is what Lucy, too, called him in her reminiscences. He and Lucy moved to Portland in 1860, and shared a long life together there. They had four children—Edward, Paul, Mary, and Henderson Brooke—and were remembered for their many contributions to the area.

Although the years were full and busy, Lucy often thought back to the humble covered wagon journey of her childhood. At the end of her life, she recorded her memories of those long-ago days. Perhaps she felt that her very character was formed by suffering from thirst and heat in the desert, by shivering under a dripping wet tree watching her father try to start a fire with steel and flint, or by inching up the rushing, icy waters of Oregon's Cow Creek canyon. She had never forgotten the magnificent green of the prairie grasslands in spring. Most of all, she remembered the hole left in their hearts when her family said good-bye forever to Lettie—a hole that began to heal with the arrival of tiny Olivia Henderson somewhere along the rough Applegate Trail. ▨

AND IN MY HEART THE MEADOW LARK STILL GAILY, SWEETLY SINGS*

The Story of Laura Elizabeth Ingalls

Silver-haired Laura Ingalls Wilder opened the beautiful writing desk her husband, Almanzo, had made for her, and ran her hand over the smooth wood. As she gazed through the window at the red sunrise over their Missouri farm, her thoughts drifted back to the hand-hewn Wisconsin log cabin where she had been born in 1867. For years she had thought of writing a book about her pioneer girlhood. Today she would begin.

Laura remembered the long-ago times when a sturdy covered wagon took her family from one little house to the next across the Midwest. She recalled the fresh, prairie-scented breeze and her steady, reliable Pa sitting tall on the wagon seat driving the mustangs while whistling a happy tune. In her mind's eye, she could see Ma—sweet-tempered, gentle Ma—sitting beside him holding baby Carrie, and later baby Freddie, and then baby Grace. She could see her older sister

---

*From a poem Laura wrote as an adult.

Mary Amelia riding in the rocking wagon with her sunbonnet neatly tied under her chin, her blue eyes watching the wild, unspoiled grasslands she would someday not be able to see.

Laura picked up her pencil and a tablet of school paper. The years had taught her never to be wasteful, so she wrote carefully from edge to edge, leaving no margin, as she put down her memories. Little did she suspect that her story, which was revised and published in the early 1930s as *Little House in the Big Woods*, would be loved by thousands of readers—and recognized everywhere as a priceless chronicle of pioneer life. Urged on by her eager fans, Laura would write eight more books to create her "Little House" series.

The stories began when Laura was a little girl living in the isolated wooded country near Pepin, Wisconsin, on the wide Mississippi River. Every day, her parents, Charles and Caroline Ingalls, whom she called Pa and Ma, worked from dawn to dark to provide for their family. Pa hunted, fished, and cleared trees for farmland, while Ma grew a garden, cared for her little girls, preserved food, and made clothes. Life in the Big Woods was a challenge, but Ma and Pa were confident and capable, and their love for each other provided a barrier against the difficulties of the life they had chosen. Different in temperament— Pa was restless and adventurous, and always wanted to be moving west, while quiet Ma preferred settling where there were schools and churches—they agreed that they wanted the best for their daughters.

The Ingalls family moved many times by covered wagon during the 1860s and 1870s, but Laura probably didn't remember their first journey since she was only about eighteen months old when it occurred. Ma's brother, Henry Quiner (who was married to Pa's sister, Polly), and Pa had each bought eighty acres of rich prairie land in Missouri. After saying good-bye to their relatives who lived in the Big Woods, Ma and Pa boosted Laura and Mary into the wagon, and the wheels began to roll. South the families went, tiny dots

CARRIE, MARY, AND LAURA INGALLS
LAURA INGALLS WILDER HOME ASSOCIATION, MANSFIELD, MO

crossing the undulating expanse of grassland, slowly moving toward their destination. Jack, the brindle bulldog, trotted behind. Rabbits bounded out of their way, meadowlarks and prairie chickens flew up from their nests, and whole towns of gophers played in the sun.

For whatever reason, the Ingalls and Quiner families moved again the next year. The Quiners returned to the Big Woods, but Pa, Ma, and the girls continued south into today's state of Kansas. There near the Verdigris River they built their "little house on the prairie." From the stories Ma and Pa told her later, Laura wrote about their new log cabin with its split-oak floor and solid roof, and about the well Pa dug by hand. It was there her sister Caroline (Carrie) Celestia Ingalls was born in August 1870.

But there were hardships on the prairie, too. Laura described the time when she and Mary, Ma, and Pa got malaria—which we now know was caused by mosquitoes in the creek bottoms—and became delirious and so weak they could hardly lift their heads from their beds. She recalled the Osage Indians, on whose land Pa inadvertently built the cabin, who were angered by the invading settlers. She wrote of wolves, panthers, and of a dangerous prairie fire.

It wasn't long until the buyer of the Wisconsin log house sent a letter saying he wanted to return the cabin to Pa and go west. So Pa and Ma decided to load their belongings into the wagon and retrace the long route back to the Big Woods. They reunited with their relatives—and with the familiar little house under the huge, old oaks. Laura loved the cozy winter nights when the fire glowed and Pa brought out the beautiful golden-brown violin he had played since he was a teenager. The music he coaxed from its strings filled the small room and etched itself in Laura's memory. Other evenings when the chores were done, Ma, who had once been a teacher, read aloud in her soft, low voice, which could just be heard above the whistling wind outside. Laura listened carefully to her words.

By the time Laura was nearly seven, the Big Woods were slowly filling with new settlers, and game was becoming scarce. Pa wanted to go west where there was plenty of space for everyone—and where there would be no stumps to fight on his farmland. His brother, Peter, who was married to Ma's younger sister, Eliza Ann—making for a third union of the Quiner-Ingalls families—agreed. So once again, supplies were loaded, good-byes were said, and the wagons creaked out of the clearing. Peter and Eliza went only a short distance before they found a farm on Minnesota's Zumbro River and stayed behind. But Pa, Ma, Mary, Laura, and Carrie went on until they reached Plum Creek near Walnut Grove on the edge of Minnesota's prairies. There they moved into a dugout, a home excavated into the creek bank. Its roof was made of hay and willow branches covered with sod, so Laura could stand on top of the little house and think it was part of the grassy prairie. With Ma's refined touch, the little dugout was soon clean and homey with smooth, whitewashed dirt walls. Laura loved to play in the sparkling creek with Mary and pick the juicy sweet plums that grew wild along its banks. Ma and Pa gratefully enrolled Laura and Mary in school, and worked to help establish the new Congregational Church in Walnut Grove, where Pa became a trustee. In the spring, Pa built a house of lumber on the banks of Plum Creek.

It was there that the family's hopes were dashed by a terrible cloud of grasshoppers that descended from the sky just before harvest time in 1875. Pa's rich, ripe wheat crop glistened in the sun, nearly ready to be cut, when the hungry insects landed and stripped the fields bare. Then they laid their eggs in the black soil, so that the next year's crop didn't have a chance of thriving. Laura wrote that Pa left on foot, following the railroad tracks east to work the harvests in areas that hadn't been invaded. He returned with enough money to see them through the crisis.

In October, 1875, the family moved into town, for Ma was

expecting another baby, and Pa didn't want her to be far from help. Little Charles Frederick Ingalls (baby Freddie) was born on November 1, 1875. Laura, Mary, and Carrie helped with the housework and chores so that Ma could rest and tend to her new son. By then, Mary was eleven years old and had developed her sweet, patient personality and good manners. Laura was nine—a spirited, independent, and intelligent girl, who, like Pa, always felt the enticing call of the West. Carrie, six, was thin and frail, but had a sunny nature like her sisters.

In the spring, the first shoots of the new wheat crop emerged from the soil—but so did the new grasshoppers. Settlers were instructed in ways to get rid of the devastating insects, but nothing worked. Discouraged, Ma and Pa decided to load their growing family into the wagon and accept Peter and Eliza Ingalls' invitation to join them on their farm near the Mississippi River. So the little canvas-covered wagon turned its wheels east again. They would live with Peter and Eliza until a new job they had been offered, running a hotel in Burr Oak, Iowa, was ready for them.

A new worry haunted them on the farm. Nine-month-old Freddie was sick, and although the doctor came, he got even sicker. Laura remembered that "one awful day he straightened out his little body and was dead." Devastated, the family mourned together. Never again would Laura hold her sweet, tiny brother or tend to his needs. Sadly, the family moved to Iowa to become hotel keepers, but she didn't mention that unhappy time in her books.

Laura's days in Burr Oak were punctuated by measles, washing hotel dishes, and attending school. Joyfully, the family welcomed the birth of their last child, golden-haired Grace Pearl Ingalls, in 1877. Ma and Pa were not fond of hotel work, and when the opportunity presented itself, they were glad to pack their faithful old wagon and head west once again. This time they drove the horses straight back to Walnut Grove, where the grasshoppers had moved on and where some of their old friends greeted them warmly. Before long, they settled into a new house in town, and the girls started school. Laura, who turned eleven, began taking small paying jobs to help the family. They spent long, happy hours with friends, attended events at the church Ma and Pa had earlier helped establish, and thrilled to the music from Pa's fiddle, which, like the unforgettable songs he sang and the stories he told, held them all together like an invisible hand through the years. Pa became Walnut Grove's justice of the peace—he held trials in their front room—and was once again a trustee in the church.

Just as the hardships seemed over, another hit with a vengeance. In the winter of 1879, Mary became gravely ill. Her fever was so high that she was delirious, and Laura was afraid she would die. Indeed, death did seem likely. Ma or Pa cut Mary's beautiful, long hair to keep her head cooler, and they nursed her faithfully. The doctors Pa called stayed near, and although Mary slowly got well, they were unable to prevent her from permanently losing her eyesight. Mary's brave patience was an inspiration to Laura, who later wrote, "All that long time, week after week, when she could still see a little, but less every day, she had never cried." It is possible that Laura's skill as a writer was honed by the hours she spent observing the things around her and then describing them for Mary, as Pa had requested.

Pa wanted to go west again, and the opportunity came when he was offered a job working on the new railroad being constructed into Dakota Territory. With a promise to Ma that this would be their last move, he left for the wild country that forever called to him. Ma and the girls followed later, making part of the trip by rail—their first experience with the noisy, smoky trains that by then screamed across the prairie. Pa met them in the covered wagon, and they finished the journey to Silver Lake (now De Smet, South Dakota) together again.

Pa helped stake out the brand new settlement, which became the "little town on the prairie" in Laura's books. Laura thrilled to the challenges of homesteading the land Pa had chosen for their claim, where he built a tiny, tarpapered shanty, which eventually became a larger home. Strong and energetic, Laura helped with the garden, the housework, the haying, and child care. Pa planted a cottonwood sapling for each of "his girls," and today they stand as huge, leafy giants overlooking the land near the bustling town of De Smet.

The family moved into town to weather the historic, fearful winter of 1880–1881 when food supplies and fuel got low and the trains could not get through the deep snow and blinding blizzards. During the years that followed, Laura attended school along with Carrie. She grew into an educated young woman who received her teaching certificate at the age of fifteen and began teaching in a one-room school. Almanzo Wilder, a farmer born in New York, soon began courting her. Mary went to a college for the blind in Iowa where she learned, among other skills, to play the organ and to do intricate bead work, and she eventually had surgery on the nerves of her face to relieve the constant pain that bothered her. Pa worked the homestead claim and held jobs in town (sheriff, justice of the peace, school board member), while Ma continued to be a steady guiding presence at home.

Laura and Almanzo were married on August 25, 1885, when Laura was eighteen, and they moved to their own claim shanty a short distance away. Laura loved the way the sunlight streamed through the glass windows, and she loved the handcrafted shelves and drawers of her new pantry, and the freshly painted yellow floor in the front room. Their first few years together were filled with terrible hardship, balanced by the joy of a newborn daughter, whom they called Rose after the wild roses that bloomed each June on the wild grasslands. Crop failure set them back, and both Almanzo and Laura got diphtheria. Almanzo, at age thirty, was left partially paralyzed.

Although he regained movement, he had a permanent shuffle to his walk and relied upon a cane throughout his life. Then in the summer of 1889, Laura gave birth to an infant son who died. Finally, when their house burned to the ground, Laura and Almanzo decided to try life elsewhere, and they moved to Florida. It was not to their liking, so they returned to De Smet, where they rented a house in town, and both worked and saved so they could search for a place to relocate.

In the summer of 1894, Laura, Almanzo, and Rose set out in Almanzo's black painted wagon with the hens' coop fastened to the back, moving slowly south toward the rich Missouri Ozarks. Near the gullies and wooded ridges of Mansfield, Missouri, they found the farm of their dreams, which they called Rocky Ridge Farm. They bought the land and moved into its small, windowless log cabin.

Over the years, the farm grew from forty acres to two hundred. Hard work brought eventual prosperity. Almanzo built a large, comfortable house entirely from materials found on the land, and they raised chickens, pigs, goats, and cows, as well as fruit and crops of all sorts. Little Rose went to school and grew up to be a noted author and journalist. Laura began her writing career by contributing articles and essays to a local farm weekly and then to magazines. At the age of sixty-five, her first book was published; others soon followed.

Back in De Smet, Pa held true to his promise never to move again. Carrie and Grace finished their schooling and married. Grace farmed with her husband nearby, and Carrie moved to the Black Hills. Mary, who had graduated from college, remained in De Smet with Ma and Pa, living in a white frame house Pa had built on Third Street, until the end of their lives. This house now stands as a museum.

Laura and Almanzo lived out their long lives on Rocky Ridge Farm. "It is the simple things of life that make living worth while, the sweet fundamental things such as love and duty, work and rest and living close to nature," Laura said. The Wilders had an abundance of these, as they worked the land in the beautiful Ozarks.

Almanzo died of a heart attack in 1949 at the age of ninety. Laura lived on alone in the house he had built until she, too, died at age ninety on February 10, 1957. Today, children worldwide still love to read her books, and Rocky Ridge has been preserved as the Laura Ingalls Wilder Home and Museum.

From the time she was a spirited little girl dressed in old-fashioned calico and a sunbonnet that always seemed to be hanging down her back, until 1957 when she died a well-loved author, Laura Elizabeth Ingalls Wilder lived the life of a quintessential American pioneer. She brought to life Mary's sightless blue eyes, Pa's singing violin, Ma's gentle personality braced with inner fortitude, and Almanzo's determined, patient hard work. She recorded forever what it was like to travel in a covered wagon to a new home somewhere in the ever-calling West. In an unassuming little notebook crowded from margin to margin, she portrayed the warm love, the deep faith, and the intense courage, honesty, and optimism that carried her and her family through blindness, fire, sickness, storms, grasshoppers, and death—and left them strong and self-sufficient in the end. ▨

A CHILD BRIDE

The Story of Mary Perry

Young Mary Perry sat on a sun-warmed boulder and looked across the new, green grass at her mother's log cabin. She was thankful that their devastating wagon trip to western Washington was over. Here in the sunshine with songbirds chirping in the undergrowth, she could almost put their harrowing journey out of her mind. The air was fresh from last night's rain; she could smell the saltwater of nearby Puget Sound. Mary dug her bare toes into the warm mud and wished for a piece of bread. She and her oldest brother earned the family's food by herding sheep for the Hudson's Bay Company, but their allotment of salt salmon and potatoes got tiresome. Occasionally the company gave them a pan of flour, too, but the warm, delicious bread Mary's mother would bake was gone before they knew it. It was a hard life for the four fatherless Perry children.

When Mr. and Mrs. Walter Perry and their family started west from their Iowa farm in April 1854, they planned to go only as far as the rich prairies of Nebraska. But the wagon train they joined was going to Oregon Territory, and Walter Perry was persuaded to take his family there instead. Mary was eight years old. Like many children her age, she probably enjoyed the first part of the long trip. Perhaps, like others, she was allowed to skip along beside the slow wagon and feel the soft dust under her feet, or catch crayfish in the rivers where they stopped for the night. Maybe it was her chore to fetch water, giving her an excuse to explore the shady riverbanks or hold up her handsewn skirts and wade into the gently tugging current. Perhaps her mother sometimes asked her to gather serviceberries or look for wild goose eggs along the riverbanks. One thing is certain: However she and her siblings spent their time on the trail, nothing could have prepared them for what lay ahead.

By the 1850s, the American Indian tribes of the West were angry with the thousands of emigrants traveling through their lands. They watched, alarmed, as new settlers built wagon roads, forts, and settlements, and hunted the once-plentiful game. Bison, so vital to the Indian way of life, were beginning to disappear at a startling rate. Troubled tribal leaders urged their people to take action, which they did in many different ways. Some, as the Perrys soon discovered, discouraged emigration by burning the grasses along the westward trails so there was no forage for the travelers' oxen. Some decided simply to trade with the emigrants, while others chose to fight them, burn their wagons, or take their livestock.

For the first four or five months, the Perrys' trip must have been uneventful, because Mary's reminiscences, which she wrote later in her life, tell little about it, not even which overland trail the party chose. But with swift suddenness, somewhere in today's state of Idaho, tragedy struck.

The wagon train had split into three smaller groups because, due to the burned grasses, there wasn't enough forage for the oxen if so many traveled together. Mary's group consisted of just four wagons. She wrote that on that fateful late summer morning, "Indians were discovered coming out of a canyon in great numbers, the foremost afoot, and apparently unarmed, followed by mounted Indians armed with guns." Two white men led the Indians toward the wagons. At first, the parties seemed interested in trading, but soon conflict ensued. In the resulting gunfire, Mary's father, her uncle, and the family's teamster were shot. Mary's uncle died immediately, and the teamster lived only until the next morning. Walter Perry, fatally injured, was cared for by his family as he lay dying in the wagon.

He had suffered a gunshot wound through his lungs. Little Mary remembered his unimaginable agony, and how he begged to be put out of his misery. He died on the evening of the fourth day and was buried near the trail, leaving Mrs. Perry a widow with four children in the wilderness.

Devastated, the Perrys pressed on, but their trials were not over. They overtook the second segment of their earlier wagon train, and a few days later, came upon another horrible scene. Their companions in the third group had been killed in a similar manner, except for two young boys who escaped. Mary wrote that they "stopped long enough to dig trenches and rude graves for the burial. . . . " It was a desperate week, one that Mary remembered all her life.

The frightened emigrants had no choice but to press on. Again the party had to split up. Many of the wagons went on to Oregon, but the Perrys and several other families, for reasons unknown, chose to travel toward Puget Sound. Mary remembered their trip over the wild Cascade Mountains at Natchez Pass, where the wagons had to be tied to strong trees with sturdy ropes and carefully inched down the steep places. "Our course," Mary wrote, "was down the Natchez River, which we had to cross sixty-two times in one day." Finally, in October 1854, the group reached its destination. Mrs. Perry moved her children into a small, windowless log cabin with a dirt floor about ten miles south of today's city of Tacoma. The rude cabin was only half covered by a roof. That is where the family ate and slept, but

EMIGRANTS AT THE GATES POST OFFICE, NEBRASKA
NEBRASKA STATE HISTORICAL SOCIETY

Mrs. Perry cooked in the open section where the continual rain fell. Mary's reminiscences do not tell the details, but a few weeks later, her mother found a "comfortable log cabin" on a donation land claim nearby on American Lake, and it became the family's new home.

Herding sheep with her brother must have been an unpleasant task for Mary, but it was necessary to help keep the family fed. Day after day, probably in the gray Puget Sound drizzle, the two were outdoors protecting the wet animals from harm. In winter, Mary would shiver inside her cold shawl, wishing she could be back in the cozy log house by the warm fire. Perhaps she got bored with the monotony of her job, or worried when, as she mentions briefly in her memoirs, she and her brother were "questioned by the Indians." It is likely that she was also frightened by the wild animals—coyotes and cougars—that almost certainly stalked the herd. Perhaps she and her brother also were expected to milk the family cows that had made the long journey west with them.

Mrs. Perry, meanwhile, traded butter with the Indians for clams and oysters, and supported her family as well as she could. Her unshakeable faith in God helped her through the many difficult times. In 1858 she married Sergeant John Cronin, whom Mary remembered as being very kind to the children when he was sober, but who was "abusive and cruel" when he was drinking, as he often was. During these times, the children frequently went to a nearby neighbor's home "for protection."

Some historians believe that Mary was looking for a way to escape the hardships of her life when she met Andrew J. Frost, who had come to Washington ten years before the Perrys arrived. Although her memoirs tell nothing of their meeting or courtship, or even his livelihood, Mary married him on May 8, 1859. She was thirteen years old.

Mary's writings were as short as her childhood, but they hold a few clues about the rest of her life. She and her husband had eight children, six of whom survived: three boys and three girls. She named one of her sons Walter G. after her father, whose life and tragic death lived in her memory. She and Andrew Frost were married fifty years. They lived most of that time in Washington, which reached statehood in 1889.

Did thirteen-year-old Mary, with her mother's blessing, joyously dance with her new husband on her wedding day, or was it a convenient marriage of simple, clear purpose as historians suggest? Her reminiscences don't tell us, but her story is unusual. While many girls wed early on the frontier, most waited until they were fifteen or sixteen years old. Mary, in contrast, was barely past childhood. It is quite possible that her unusual girlhood gave her the rare maturity to cope with a very early marriage and the subsequent life of a pioneer woman. But perhaps she saw her union with Andrew Frost as a chance to create a secure new life for herself, free from dull sheep, monotonous salt salmon, the cruelty of her often drunk stepfather, and the vivid trail memories that doubtless haunted her thoughts and dreams. ▨

ORPHANED ON THE OREGON TRAIL

The Story of Catherine Sager

If Henry and Naomi Sager could have foreseen the hardships and tragedies that awaited their family on the Oregon Trail, they never would have left their western Missouri cabin that spring. But in April 1844, they set out in a large covered wagon with their six children, bound for the rich land and healthful climate of Oregon. It was nine-year-old Catherine who remembered their dramatic and disastrous journey best. Later in life, she wrote about her experiences in a memoir. Two of her younger sisters, Elizabeth Marie, who was seven, and Matilda Jane, five, also later wrote accounts of the trip. (Two-year-old Hannah Louise Sager was too young to remember.) Their story was one of the saddest—but most triumphant—of the western trails.

The trip began routinely with the crossing of the great Missouri River. Once they were safely over, a seventy-two-unit wagon train was organized, a man named William Shaw was elected captain, and the company began its slow progress along the banks of the Platte River in today's state of Nebraska. "Oh, those first encampments! How the children did enjoy them!" Catherine wrote later in her life.

Most likely, she and her older brothers (John, about thirteen, and Francis, twelve) and her three younger sisters played with the other children of the wagon train as twilight fell across the prairie. Campfires crackled while some of the travelers tuned their musical instruments for an evening of singing or dancing. But the long, unusually wet spring days in the wagon were unpleasant for the children because the constant rocking gave them motion sickness. They became adept at quickly jumping out of the moving wagon so they could walk alongside the plodding oxen.

Late in May, the children were surprised when another little sister was born. The infant was named Rosanna, and, since their mother Naomi Sager was not well, Catherine almost certainly helped care for the baby, perhaps comforting her cries, or even bathing her in river water warmed over the fire. The wagons made slow but steady progress during June and July. Few pioneers had traveled the trail before, and the road was rough and crude. Twice accidents befell the family—once the wagon overturned, knocking Naomi unconscious, and another time the children's bed covers caught fire as they slept in the family tent—but no lasting harm was done, and the family pressed on. The company passed through buffalo country where Henry Sager was thrilled with the opportunity to hunt the huge beasts. By the first of August, the wagon train had nearly reached Fort Laramie, a distance of approximately 550 miles.

It was there that the family's first tragedy occurred. Catherine had stepped out onto the wagon tongue to jump free of the moving wagon. But as she leaped, her dress caught on an axe handle and she was thrown under the huge iron-rimmed wheels. Her horrified father quickly stopped the oxen, but it was too late. The wagon had rolled over her left leg, badly crushing it. Henry Sager set the bone with the help of a kind thirty-four-year-old German doctor from the wagon train behind them, Theophilos Dagon, but Catherine was in great

CATHERINE SAGER PRINGLE
OREGON HISTORICAL SOCIETY #883, OrHI 59558

pain and was, after that, confined to the wagon. As she lay there, uncomfortably jostling over every bump beside her mother and infant sister, surely she longed for her leg to heal so once again she could run through the soft grasses with her brothers and sisters. "Sickness had also become prevalent in the company," Catherine remembered. She indicated that several members of the wagon party died. Her father and brothers fell ill, and the family had to depend on Dr. Dagon to drive their wagon. As the company lumbered on toward the Green River in today's western Wyoming, Henry Sager became deathly ill with typhoid fever. It soon became apparent that he would die, and Catherine wrote that her father's "heart was filled with anguish" to leave his family alone. He begged Captain Shaw to watch over his wife and children and to see that they finished the journey safely. The captain promised, and Henry Sager died the next morning. He was buried on the banks of the Green River.

The family's troubles had just begun. Although the dedicated Dr. Dagon refused to leave Naomi Sager's side, feeling it was his duty to help watch over the family now, she was still sick. She decided to stop at Fort Hall in the southwest corner of what is now Idaho, exchange her livestock for horses, and pack into the nearest missionary station with her children for the winter. But her responsibilities were overwhelming, and she was grieving over her husband's death. Her health worsened. Catherine wrote that even though her mother was "consumed with fever, and afflicted with the sore mouth that was the forerunner of the fatal camp fever" (typhoid), she tried her best to fight the weakness and pain. After all, if she succumbed, her seven children would be orphaned in the wilderness. Despite her determination, however, Naomi was too weak to unpack at Fort Hall, and a short way beyond, became delirious and bedridden. The other women of the company cared for her and for the children, especially tiny Rosanna. But even with their tender nursing, Naomi died—only about a month after her husband.

Catherine's memoir does not describe the terrible, aching loss and sadness the children must have felt. Their grief was almost certainly compounded by intense fear and uncertainty. Being orphaned in the wilderness was terrifying for children on the western trails. Through their tears, Catherine and her brothers must have wondered desperately how they would cope. The two youngest children, baby Rosanna and little Hannah Louise, needed constant care. The wagon had to be driven, and food was running low. Fortunately, the other families in the wagon train, even though laden with their own cares, sprang to the children's aid, especially Captain and Mrs. Shaw, who gave gentle, affectionate care to the devastated orphans. Catherine wrote that the children were "literally adopted by the train" and that one of the travelers cared for Rosanna as if she were her own. Dr. Dagon drove the covered wagon.

Several hundred hard miles remained to their journey, and the children's ox team was weak. Captain Shaw took a day or two from the urgent travel schedule so the children's large wagon could be made into a smaller cart that could be pulled more easily. But the train was out of flour, and the weather was starting to get cold—so cold that little Hannah Louise nearly died of hypothermia one night when she wandered, crying, out of the wagon. The captain felt it would be best if the children were taken to the nearest mission and left there for the winter.

The party had by then crossed the difficult Blue Mountains, located in today's northeastern Oregon, and the closest mission was the one established by the widely known Marcus and Narcissa Whitman at Waiilatpu near the present site of Walla Walla, Washington. Captain Shaw went ahead of the train on horseback to buy food and to ask the Whitmans if they could keep the children. The hard-working couple, who had already taken on several other children, agreed, and so Captain Shaw and the good German doctor delivered the grief-stricken, disheveled Sagers to the mission. Baby Rosanna, who was very ill, was kept behind a few days until she was stronger.

Catherine recalled that her first weeks at the mission were filled with tears. Although Narcissa Whitman immediately cleaned and fed the children, and talked with them gently in her pleasant, musical voice, Catherine was still traumatized by losing both her parents, and she found it hard being sent to live among strangers, kind as they were. Her leg was not yet healed so she could not join her brothers and sisters in exploring the mission. She sat indoors rocking her baby sister (whose name was changed to Henrietta Naomi, in honor of both her parents) in a cradle and sewing, while slowly she adjusted to her new home and began to feel comfortable with Dr. and Mrs. Whitman.

Marcus and Narcissa Whitman were New Englanders, the famous, dedicated missionaries who had crossed the Rockies in 1836 to spread their Presbyterian faith among the native peoples of the West. Narcissa had been one of the first two white women to venture into the wilderness, and she had traveled almost four thousand miles overland, nearly all on horseback since no wagon trails existed at that early date. The missionaries had labored to establish their elaborate settlement with its mill, garden, irrigation ditches, blacksmith's shop, orchard, and house, and had built good communications with the Indians, especially the nearby Cayuse.

The Whitmans had very disciplined ideas about raising children. For the next three years the Sager orphans lived at the mission under their strict rules and loving care. The days settled into a routine. "We had certain things to do at a certain hour," wrote Matilda Sager, Catherine's sister. Every morning and evening, in addition to preparing meals and cleaning up, there was family worship. Each child learned a daily Scripture verse and attended the mission school. They helped with the chores, and each had to tend a section of the large vegetable garden, which was grown partly to supply food for passing emigrants. Sometimes they swam in the river, had singing lessons, or took long walks with Narcissa to study plant life. Matilda wrote that they were allowed to play in the water with hollowed-out watermelons for boats. "Still," she wrote, "discipline was strict and when we were told to do a thing, no matter what, we went." The children grew to love the Whitmans, calling them "mother" and "father" and respecting their wishes. Under Narcissa's expert care, Catherine's leg healed until she could walk normally again, and baby Henrietta grew into a healthy, well-loved child. The two boys approached manhood under the careful tutelage of Dr. Whitman, who became the children's legal guardian.

But more trouble was in store for them, this time more traumatic than anything they had yet experienced. The Whitmans had worked hard with the surrounding groups of Cayuse people, but in 1847 an unfortunate epidemic of measles arrived with the wagon travelers who were continually stopping at the mission. Measles were deadly and contagious, and soon the epidemic spread not only throughout the mission but also to the Cayuse villages. Never having been exposed to the disease before, the Cayuse were especially hard-hit. Large numbers of their people began dying, and although the Whitmans tried to help care for them, there was little they could do to stop the terrible disease. At the same time, rumors that the Whitmans had purposefully spread the epidemic as part of a plot to take over their land began to disturb the Cayuse. Tribal leaders held councils, deliberating. Were the missionaries to blame? Should they be killed? The Whitmans knew of these deliberations and were, of course, troubled by them. They thought seriously about closing the mission the following spring. Marcus was aware that the outcome of Cayuse anger could be his death.

Still it was a horrible shock when the possibility became reality. On November 29, 1847, the natives, now convinced that the Whitmans were at the heart of their troubles, came to the mission. On that terrible, bloody afternoon, they killed both missionaries, the young Sager brothers—sixteen-year-old John and fifteen-year-old Francis—and several of the other mission settlers. Elizabeth Sager later wrote that she and her sisters were "doomed to witness what I pray I may never behold again. . . . It makes my blood run cold to think of it." The sisters hid in the attic, nearly paralyzed with fear, shock, and sadness.

The girls were desperately sick with both measles and trauma. Five days after the Whitmans were killed, Hannah Louise Sager died. Only Catherine, Elizabeth, Matilda, and Henrietta Naomi were left, and, amid their terror for their own lives, they grieved deeply over the loss of their three beloved siblings and their devoted adopted parents. Along with the other women and children from the mission who had survived the killings, the girls were taken captive by the Cayuse.

A few weeks later, Peter Skene Ogden, a respected representative of the Hudson's Bay Company, was able to purchase the captives from the Cayuse with a large load of blankets, cotton shirts, guns, ammunition, flints, and tobacco brought from Fort Vancouver. They were taken to Fort Walla Walla, and from there traveled in open boats down the Columbia River to Fort Vancouver and later to Oregon City—the end of the Oregon Trail near today's city of Portland. As Catherine and her three sisters floated the silver waters of the Columbia, no doubt they said fervent prayers of thanks for the end of their ordeal—and again cried anguished tears for their losses.

The girls found separate homes among the settlers. Elizabeth lived with six different families in the seven years between her arrival in the Willamette Valley and her marriage, and Henrietta, too, was reportedly transferred from family to family. The other girls were placed in more permanent homes, although Matilda escaped her unhappy situation by marrying a thirty-one-year-old miner at the age of fifteen. Catherine, who at thirteen was small but capable and mature, was taken in by the superintendent of a Methodist mission, Reverend William M. Roberts and his wife. They "did well by me," Catherine reported later, and she appreciated the home life they offered her. During this time, she received a letter through the Salem post office giving her address as "Somewhere in Oregon." It was from her father's brother in the East, who had been able to trace his long-lost nieces to that area. Catherine and her sisters had yearned to be in touch with someone related to them by blood, and they excitedly wrote back, asking questions about their family, and hoping for a daguerreotype and locks of hair as keepsakes.

At sixteen, Catherine married Clark Spencer Pringle, who became a Methodist circuit rider. The couple settled four miles from Salem, Oregon. Catherine sent for Elizabeth and Henrietta to come live with them, and so for the next few years the three sisters were together again. Matilda lived two days' travel away.

Eventually, Henrietta and Elizabeth married and moved on. As the years passed, Catherine became the skillful mother of eight children. She was a calm, kind person with a sense of humor, and she and Clark spent many busy years raising their family. As Catherine grew older, she realized that her childhood memories, harsh as they were, shed light on events that would go down in history, so she began giving talks around the Pacific Northwest about the early Oregon Trail, and about Marcus and Narcissa Whitman and the events that ended their lives. She also wrote down her own saga.

The triumph of Catherine Sager and her sisters did, indeed, go down in history. Their story has been told many times, sometimes incorrectly, but always with admiration for their success and resilience.

Catherine went on to live a full, courageous life, helping to settle the West and to preserve its history. No doubt the haunting memories lived with her forever. But her writings, which she called "my humble efforts," and those of her sisters, are among the most important historical documents existing today about the events they witnessed on their long journey west. Catherine's life ended on August 10, 1919, at the home of her youngest daughter in Spokane, Washington. She was seventy-five years old, a tiny, fragile-looking woman, but as her granddaughter described her, "oh, so capable." Capable is an apt word for this strong and resilient pioneer. Her life story—especially her remarkable survival of an almost unbearable childhood—is an inspiring event in American history that clearly brings perspective to our lives today. ■

One Stew Kettle
to Her Name

The Story of Martha Ann Morrison

John Minto scrambled up a steep bank and looked back over the wagon train bound for Oregon. It was a pretty sight. The white canvas wagon covers flapped in the warm breeze as the train wound its way toward the sparkling Green River. He was glad to see that young Martha Ann Morrison was walking along beside her family's two covered wagons, her patched dress blowing gracefully in the wind. Martha had been sick with camp fever for part of the trip, but now she looked healthy again. Even from a distance, her dark hair shone in the afternoon sunshine and her step was lively. Twenty-one-year-old John, whom Martha's father had hired to help see the family over the harsh Oregon Trail, knew that when she was old enough he would ask this spirited, practical girl to be his wife.

But for now, John had other concerns. Returning to the wagons from his hillside viewpoint, he found that one of the men in the party who was sick with typhoid needed someone to care for him during the long night ahead. Always willing to help, John volunteered. Perhaps he could nurse Henry Sager back to health so that frail Naomi Sager and the couple's seven children would not be left to cope with the rigors of the overland trail without him. As evening fell, he began his vigil. After a long, physically exhausting day on the road, it was difficult to stay awake, and John had to make himself stay watchful. The hours dragged by while he did everything he could to help, but by morning he knew it was no use. Henry Sager would die that day.

The travelers had to press on. Wilson and Nancy Morrison, Martha's parents, realized the wagon train needed to keep moving steadily in order to reach Oregon country before winter. They looked forward to helping settle the pleasant Willamette Valley for the United States. Like some of the other westward travelers, they had left Missouri partly because they wanted to get away from the rampant slavery that surrounded them in the South, and partly because they wished to create a better life for themselves and their six children: Martha (twelve), Mary Ann (ten), John (nine), Hanna (five), Thomas (three), and James Franklin (one). Nancy Morrison was expecting a seventh child and had not been well. So as the wagons strained along the rutted, muddy Oregon Trail, Martha helped as much as she could. She almost certainly watched the youngest children to make sure they were safe from the roaring streams, hot campfires, the oxen's heavy hooves, poisonous berries, loaded guns, and the wolves they often saw. And she helped with the cooking. Usually food preparation on the road was drudgery, but Martha took her turn to gather fuel (sticks and logs if the travelers were in wooded country, dried buffalo dung or sagebrush if they were not), to stir the Dutch oven full of bubbling beans, or to measure the precious, savory coffee into the big coffeepot.

Sometimes, as Martha walked along hour after hour beside the laboring cattle, she had time to think about the refinements of the settlements they had left behind. She was ashamed of her coarse, bare feet. But shoes wore out quickly on a rough overland journey like this. By now the soles of her feet were so tough and calloused that she could walk almost comfortably if she watched for thorns, wasps, and rattlesnakes. Some days, though, walking was a luxury. Being the oldest child in the family, she often had to drive the plodding cattle pulling the massive wagons, and other times she was needed to follow behind and help herd the loose stock animals.

Was it her imagination, or did handsome John Minto glance her way now and then? She liked the energetic, competent young man her family depended on to help get them through to Oregon. The trip from their Missouri farm had been difficult so far. The rains of 1844 were some of the heaviest in the nation's history, and the family had been continually wet, cold, and muddy. Rushing high streams had delayed their progress. But somehow through it all, John had stayed cheerful, whistling about his work and enjoying the spectacular beauty of the landscape. He was educated, too. In his spare time he wrote poetry—he was a great admirer of the poet Robert Burns—and kept a lengthy journal, and he entertained the others with his singing.

John's diary, written in small, neat script, recorded details about huge herds of bison that covered the plains, the sea of lush grasses made taller and thicker by the rain, immense flocks of passenger pigeons, encounters with the native peoples, the lives of his fellow travelers, and his interest in Martha. She, too, recorded the journey's events during an interview that was written down when she was in her thirties. Her vivid oral history brought her journey alive.

It wasn't until the last of August that the wagon train reached Fort Bridger, located in the lower southwest corner of today's state of Wyoming. Food was running low, and the travelers were in danger of encountering storms and heavy snow before the journey's end. John Minto and two others, clearly seeing the danger, asked to go ahead to the settlements to alert them to the problems. Meanwhile, the Morrisons and their wagon train—with Martha's father as captain—made slow headway day after day. The trek was exhausting but mostly

MARTHA ANN MORRISON WITH HUSBAND, JOHN MINTO,
AND FIRST CHILD
OREGON HISTORICAL SOCIETY #753-A, OrHi 37784

uneventful until the tired travelers finally reached a windy stopping place near The Dalles (a place of rocky rapids) on the wide Columbia River two hundred miles upstream from the Pacific Coast. By then it was December. The wind blew constantly, driving the chill into the wagon and under the family's threadbare clothes. The food was gone. Mrs. Morrison was forced to trade her only spare dress to the Indians for a peck of potatoes, which were soon consumed by her ravenous family. Fatigued and discouraged, the weary emigrants watched the endless drizzle falling from the gray skies.

It was then that John Minto and his partners appeared, slogging upriver with fresh provisions and a boat sent from the settlements. We can only imagine the gratitude with which the Morrisons greeted the tired young men who had devotedly hauled the small French *bateau* against the powerful current all the way from Fort Vancouver, a distance of about seventy-five miles. Perhaps the glow Martha felt in her heart for Johnny Minto burst into flame that day.

"All the goods we had in the world were put into a little canoe, including all the children. . . ." reported Martha later, as they abandoned their wagon and took to the river. The craft was in danger of overturning in the cold, turbulent waters. Storms battered the travelers with driving rain. John Minto described one gale that "was the most awful effect of wind that I have ever seen." Forced ashore, the children crouched under an old quilt and tried to stay warm, while wind howled and "blew the logs off the fire," Martha remembered. When the weather broke, the trip downstream resumed. The party skirted waterfalls and camped night after night on the wet shores. It seemed an endless journey, but as January ended and February began, they neared their final destination: the Clatsop Plains at the mouth of the mighty Columbia.

There was no other way to reach the farmland Mr. Morrison selected for their new home except to wade through "two tremendous swamps" glutted with fallen trees and undergrowth. Nancy Morrison and her daughters held their skirts high to avoid the knee-deep mud and briars. "Mother was a very fleshy woman," Martha reported, "and it was a terrible job for her to get through," especially since she was pregnant and also carrying their toddler on her hip. The family settled into a little cabin that was open to the winter weather. "We were just as poor as we could be," Martha said. "We literally had nothing. . . ." Mr. Morrison, generous to a fault, had shared nearly all their goods with other families in need, but now his own was nearly destitute. "We made patched dresses of all colors—even our stockings were many-colored." Martha said. She told of picking and trading ripe cranberries for a piece of poor blue fabric, but shoes and stockings were not to be had.

Before long, John Minto left to retrieve the cattle that the emigrants had left behind when they boarded the boat near The Dalles. That done, his contract with Mr. Morrison was fulfilled. He had seen the family and its livestock safely through to Oregon country, and was now free to do as he wished. Realizing that Martha was still too young for marriage, John worked at whatever jobs came his way, waiting until the day they could be married.

That day came two years later on July 8, 1847, when Martha was fifteen and her parents consented to the wedding. The ceremony was only the second to be held in the little Clatsop Plains schoolhouse, and the new couple's honeymoon was a week-long canoe trip to the site of Salem, Oregon, where they set up housekeeping. Once again, they were desperately poor, but full of hope, love, and ambition. "When I went to housekeeping, I had just one stew kettle that belonged to a stove, but there was no thought of a stove; we had that kettle to make coffee, or bread, or to fry meat, for we had not even a frying pan," Martha recalled. The young couple had two sheets, which she cut up to make shirts for her new husband. Seventy-five cents was "every cent of money we had for two or three years," Martha recalled. People told them they should return to the East where life was easier, but Martha indignantly wondered how they were supposed to do that without a wagon, cattle, or even supplies.

Slowly, with hard work and determination, their situation improved. Land was abundant, and they acquired 640 beautiful, rich acres—320 acres each through donation land claims. As time passed, they welcomed their first child, John W., and then their daughter, Mary Ellen. John left his family briefly to travel to California during the gold rush and returned with enough wealth to plant some of their acreage with fine varieties of apples, pears, plums, peaches, and cherries. He became an expert at raising animals, especially Merino sheep, and the family began to prosper.

Eventually, eight children were born to Martha and John. When Martha's health started to fail, they purchased more land in the shady foothills of the cool Cascade Mountains where they camped each summer with their family. In the crisp, clear air her strength improved. In 1859—eleven years after becoming an official United States Territory—Oregon became a state. John was elected to the state House of Representatives for four sessions throughout the latter part of the century. Amid his statesman's duties, he continued to write, often dedicating his poems to Martha, the love of his life. Martha became known as an early feminist and supporter of women's rights. When she died in 1904 in her early seventies, her family remembered her warmth and kindness, her stoic acceptance of the things she could not change, and her spirited demeanor. John lived to the age of ninety-two, active to the end with his many friends, his children and their families, and his wide interests.

Today, in and around the city of Salem, there are several landmarks that bear the Minto name. They remind us of this strong, resilient couple who overcame destitution with work, cheerfulness, a little luck, and most of all, abiding love—and who together created a strong founding family for the capital city of their promised land. ▨

TROUBLE ON THE GILA TRAIL
The Stories of Susan Thompson and Olive Oatman

S eventeen-year-old Susan Thompson tuned up her violin, which glowed a rich honey-brown in the evening sunset. Tonight her fellow wagon travelers would dance to her lively tunes under the glittering stars hanging low over the Kansas prairie. Their thirty covered wagons stood near, ready to roll westward again at the first hint of dawn. For now, the men hastened to finish their evening chores, and the women chatted amiably as they washed the supper dishes and pitched the sleeping tents in the tall grass. The scent of campfire smoke filled the air.

Among the party's travelers were Susan's friends, Lucy and Olive Oatman, who were going west with their parents and siblings. Lucy was seventeen and Olive was younger, about thirteen. The families had joined with other westward travelers in Independence, Missouri, to form a wagon train and had finally started out over the Kansas plains in midsummer. At first, the three girls thought the trip was an adventure, with "plenty of frolic," as Susan wrote in her later memoirs. The young people enjoyed the wagon stops during the day when foot races were held and great, arcing swings were hung from overhanging tree boughs. As night fell, the older boys and girls teased and flirted with one another while they gathered around campfires with the others to dance, play games, and tell stories. Slowly the party wended its way southwest across Kansas and down the long Arkansas River, moving toward its destination. The group hoped to establish a new American colony on the Gulf of California, where the climate was said to be mild and pleasant year-round.

As the company traveled closer to New Mexico, though, the travelers became tense. This was the Santa Fe Trail, the year was 1850, and they were deep in Apache country. The Apaches were among the masters of the Southwest whose presence struck fear into the hearts of westward emigrants, partly because of their many successful raids on settlements and wagon companies. Royce Oatman, Lucy and Olive's father who was captain of their group, was "fully aware of the peril" Susan remembered. Instead of the carefree evenings the party had enjoyed earlier, he now had the wagons form a tight, guarded circle each night with the stock animals corralled inside.

Susan and her friends, like many young people of the overland trails, most likely didn't realize the extent of the danger. Susan wrote about one night when she and Lucy realized they had forgotten to fill the water pails for morning, so in order to avoid being scolded, they slipped past the guard and hurried down to the river, despite an Apache camp visible across the water. When they heard a rustling noise, they clung together "remembering all too late the warnings we had heard of the fearful Apache" and were enormously relieved when they discovered that the noise came from another wagon traveler also getting water.

The pioneers pressed on, heading deeper into the dry wilderness. Discord started to divide the party, but they continued day after day along the dusty trail. Several weeks later, by then growing weary of the strain, the company reached a small stopover in northern New Mexico. There a choice had to be made. Should the company stay on the well-established trail, which was glutted with deep sand, or should they try a new, less sandy route, which had never before been traveled by a wagon party? Opinions were mixed, and finally the party decided to split up. The majority stayed on the old road, but the Oatmans and Thompsons, along with five other families, resolved to try the new way. No doubt Susan, Lucy, and Olive rejoiced that their families decided to stay together so they could continue to enjoy each others' company.

They set off into the unknown. In contrast to the green farms they had been accustomed to back home in Iowa, this new land seemed foreign indeed with its rocky terrain, dry climate, and strange vegetation. The untried road slowed them down, because it was difficult to find places for the big wagons to safely ford the streams. Gone from Susan's memoirs are mentions of violin tunes and lively dances, foot races and flirting. Instead she wrote of tying heavy logs to the backs of their wagons to slow their descent in treacherously steep spots, and of learning to make some small pink flowers into a quinine-like medicine. She spoke of one incident when the Apaches stampeded their animals and drove off "seventeen head of stock, which we could ill afford to lose. . . ."

The wagons moved nearly due south to follow the Rio Grande. Despite their southern route, snowstorms delayed them as autumn faded into winter. Supplies were running low. The families hoped to restock when they reached the small settlement of Santa Cruz just south of today's Mexican border. Unfortunately, raids had reduced supplies there to almost nothing, so the small party pushed northwest toward Tucson. Each traveler was allowed only a biscuit and a half per day and a portion of whatever game could be shot, including hawks and coyotes. Finally, with the strain taking its toll, the small group reached Tucson, where Susan celebrated her eighteenth birthday on January 8, 1851, exactly eight months after the family had started out from Iowa. She and her female companions were the first white women to travel to the small town, and Susan felt the settlers there were not quick to accept the newcomers. She reported that she won their favor by mixing a poultice to draw a painful mesquite thorn from a Mexican settler's foot. From then on, their party was welcomed, and the man whose foot she had healed rented them a house temporarily so they could rest for a few weeks and stock up on needed supplies.

It was there that the stories of Susan Thompson and the Oatman girls diverged. Royce Oatman, Lucy and Olive's father, felt it was best to push on immediately to Fort Yuma—near the southernmost point in the border between today's California and Arizona—which was relatively close to their final destination. Undoubtedly the two sisters wished to remain behind with Susan, their faithful trail companion for hundreds of miles. But it was not to be. After a sad good-bye, the Oatmans and a few others resumed their slow travel, by then over the Gila Trail, leaving Susan and her family behind.

The Oatman party inched through the Sonoran Desert toward Fort Yuma. Thirteen-year-old Olive—who later wrote a personal narrative about her experiences—didn't like that "most dismal, desolate, and unfruitful" part of the trail. Stopping at some friendly Pima Indian villages near present-day Phoenix, Arizona, the Oatmans faced a dilemma. Should they stay with the Pimas where the Apache were likely to attack and food was very scarce, or should they push on through the dangerous country ahead and try to reach Fort Yuma? Their traveling companions decided to stay, but Royce Oatman concluded it was safer to try to reach the fort. Despite the dangers of traveling alone, the family set out. Their oxen were nearly spent, and deep sand hindered their travel. But they labored on until they reached a spot less than one hundred miles from Fort Yuma, where they came to a steep hill. The worn-out oxen could not pull the wagons up, so the family unloaded their belongings to lighten the load. Some historical accounts say that Mrs. Oatman was expecting a child and went into labor in that remote, lonesome spot. At any rate, the family stopped, distracted from its usual watchfulness. There in the hot spring sunshine, tragedy struck.

When the family looked up, a band of what Olive later said were Apaches had surrounded the wagons. In spite of the fact that they indicated friendship, Royce knew at once his family was in trouble. The leaders asked for food, and the Oatmans gave them a small amount of their meager supply. If the family offered more, they themselves would surely starve before they could reach the fort, and so when the Indians asked, Royce refused. Angered, they withdrew for a short conference, and then suddenly attacked. Within minutes, Olive's parents, Lucy, and three of the other children were killed. The oldest boy, Lorenzo, was injured and left for dead, and Olive and her seven-year-old sister Mary Ann were taken captive. The wagon was stripped of its contents.

Who can imagine what thoughts crossed Olive's mind as she and little Mary Ann stumbled barefoot mile after mile, driven by their captors? Who can comprehend her grief and trauma at losing her family, and her extreme fear as she was hurried along by these strange men whose language she did not speak and whose ways she did not understand? Little Mary Ann was devastated and was becoming more exhausted by the moment. Their feet were bleeding. Expecting to be killed, Olive prayed fervently to God for help.

Lorenzo regained consciousness the next morning as the sun beat down on him. Dazed and bleeding, he hobbled away from the dreadful site into the desert. Three long days later, he came across the traveling companions his family had left behind at the Pima villages. Horrified, they rescued him and nursed his wounds and heard his story. Then they sent a message about the tragedy and Lorenzo's escape to the Thompsons, whom they knew would be following them soon.

In the meantime, Susan's family and their companions, by then somewhat refreshed, had started out on the trail again. The message about the Oatman fate reached them, and it was with heavy hearts and bitter tears that they passed the terrible place where their friends had died and where Olive and Mary Ann had been kidnapped. When Susan found the kindling basket of her beloved friend Lucy lying abandoned on the ground, she could hardly stand the sight, and the thought that the two girls had been taken captive was too much to bear. Grieving, the group pressed on through burning sand dunes, avoiding the rattlesnakes, scorpions, and lizards that abounded on the Gila Trail, trying to reach Fort Yuma before a similar fate overtook them. As it was, Susan's father was ill and her little sister was so wasted away that Susan wrote, "We hardly hoped for her life."

Her spirits were given a boost when, finally reaching Fort Yuma, Mrs. Thompson gave birth to a baby sister, Gila, "whom we named in honor of the river near her birthplace." Knowing that the travel-worn family was reaching the end of its endurance, Mr. Thompson promised they would make their new home "at the first place where water was to be had in abundance," Susan wrote. In spite of the loss of their friends, the family was grateful and heartened to near a final destination, and they set out again, this time with Susan scouting the trail and urging the exhausted oxen along by holding mesquite beans just out of reach. Mr. Thompson was so ill by then that he was delirious.

And so it was Susan herself who saw the family through the sand dunes to their new home. Stumbling through the baking heat, urging the dead-tired teams along with the promise of a mouthful of food, she made certain that the Thompsons completed the grueling journey. Slowly Mr. Thompson began to regain his health. Fourteen months after they started out, they arrived at a stage stop between Los Angeles and San Bernardino, where the cool waters of the San Gabriel River flowed through "masses of watercress and rushes. . . ." There they built a home of mud and sticks, and opened their doors to the many travelers who used the busy trail.

In the meantime, Olive and Mary Ann Oatman had spent their days as slaves in the camp of their nomadic captors. Conditions were primitive, food was hard to find, and the girls were expected to work hard even after they became weak with fatigue and starvation. They clung together, grief-stricken over the loss of their family, and hoping against hope they would be rescued—or that they would be killed. Olive was protective of her frail little sister as they began to learn the ways of the tribe and to understand its language. Often they talked secretly of escape, but the camp was reportedly two hundred miles from the nearest emigrant trail—an impossible distance in their condition, even if they had known the way. And so a year passed with the girls in strict captivity.

It was then that their captors traded them to the more gentle Mohave Indians, and the girls were moved to a new camp, still far from any emigrant trails or settlements. There the chief took them into his family. Tragically, a famine struck the Mohave people, and after enduring near starvation for many months, little Mary Ann died. Olive was left alone. Unable to contain her grief, she sank for a time into a deep depression. The chief's compassionate wife and daughter, however, brought her nourishment in the midst of the famine and showed her other kindnesses. Olive was allowed to start her own garden, and the Indian women watched over her crops when Olive went far afield searching for roots and nuts to eat. She made a sort of altar where Mary Ann's body was buried and went there often to pray.

Several years passed. In the tradition of the Mohaves, Olive was tattooed on her chin with vertical black lines made by pressing carbonized rock powder into cuts in her fair skin. By then she was a

OLIVE OATMAN
IN THE FASHION OF MOHAVE WOMEN,
OLIVE WAS TATTOOED ON HER CHIN AND ARMS.
ARIZONA HISTORICAL SOCIETY/TUCSON, AHS# 1927

beautiful young woman, and some accounts say that she was married to the chief's son, and became the mother of two small boys.

Olive was unaware that Lorenzo had survived the long-ago attack on their family. In fact, he made his home with Susan Thompson, who was by then safely settled in California and married to a man named David Lewis. As Lorenzo grew into adulthood, he never forgot seeing his sisters taken captive by the Apaches, and he began to search for them. He caught word of a white girl living among the Mohaves and knew she could be one of his sisters. Reports say he arranged for her capture with the help of a Yuma Indian named Francisco and the officers at Fort Yuma.

Francisco negotiated long and hard with the Mohaves for Olive's release and was finally successful. He and Olive started on foot to Fort Yuma, with the chief's daughter accompanying them. As they walked the ten days' journey, was Olive rejoicing to be leaving the Mohave camp and returning to those she had loved in an earlier life? Or did her heart remain with her new civilization and the wilderness life that had become so familiar to her over the past five years? In her later writings, she confessed to having mixed feelings: "Anxious as I was to regain my liberty:—yet—I could not leave the wilde mountain home without a struggle."

She arrived at the fort dressed in a bark skirt, with dark tattoos on her chin. After so long a time in such different surroundings, even the English language had faded from Olive's mind, and at first she had a difficult time remembering it.

Accounts differ, but historians generally agree that she was reunited with her brother and then went to live with either her friend Susan Thompson Lewis or Susan's parents for a time. Abruptly changing cultures must have been extremely difficult for her because Susan noted in her memoirs that Olive was often unhappy. "In time we erased the tatoo marks from her face but we could not erase the wild life from her heart," she wrote.

It is uncertain if Olive ever completely lost her Mohave tattoos or her half-yearning for her "wilde mountain home." Later she joined relatives in Oregon, and, according to Susan's memoirs, eventually married a banker. She traveled, sometimes giving talks about her years of captivity, attended a California university for a time, and wrote down her experiences. Susan lived out her life in California, remarrying after her husband passed away, and reportedly becoming the mother of eight children.

Today the overland trails are mostly highways. But somewhere in the vast, dry desert of Arizona is a place once called "Oatman Flat," a reminder of the tragedy that happened there. As we speed by in air-conditioned cars, we can scarcely imagine the difficulty of passing that way in a covered wagon, miring in sand, rationing biscuits, laboring ahead in spite of sickness and thirst, and watching over every rise for danger. Yet Susan Thompson and Olive Oatman's girlhood friendship and pioneer spirit survived the events that separated them, and they both went on to live resourceful lives. Perhaps that was their victory over the long and unforgiving way west and the trouble on the Gila Trail. ▨

BIBLIOGRAPHY

General Sources:

Florin, Lambert. *Western Wagon Wheels.* Seattle: Superior Publishing Company, 1970.

Horn, Huston. *The Pioneers.* Time-Life Books—The Old West Books. New York: Time-Life Books, 1979.

Reader's Digest Association, Inc. *Story of the Great American West.* Pleasantville, N.Y.: Reader's Digest Association, Inc., 1977.

Reiter, Joan Swallow. *The Women.* Time-Life Books—The Old West Books. Alexandria, Va.: Time-Life Books, 1979.

Schlissel, Lillian. *Women's Diaries of the Westward Journey.* New York: Schocken Books, 1982.

Werner, Emmy E. *Pioneer Children on the Journey West.* Boulder, San Francisco, and Oxford: Westview Press, 1995.

West, Elliot. *Growing Up with the Country: Childhood on the Far Western Frontier.* Albuquerque: University of New Mexico Press, 1989.

Virginia Reed:

Holmes, Kenneth L., ed. and comp. *Covered Wagon Women: Diaries and Letters from the Western Trails 1840–1890.* Vol. 1. Glendale, Calif.: The Arthur H. Clark Company, 1983. [This volume includes the letters of Tamsen E. Donner and Virginia Elizabeth B. Reed.]

Stewart, George R. Jr., *Ordeal by Hunger: The Story of the Donner Party*. New York: Henry Holt Company, 1936.

Zeinert, Karen, ed. *Across the Plains in the Donner Party*. North Haven, Conn.: Linnet Books, 1996.

Sallie Hester:

Hester, Sallie. "The Diary of a Pioneer Girl: The Adventures of Sallie Hester, Aged Twelve, in a Trip Overland in 1849." In *Covered Wagon Women: Diaries and Letters from the Western Trails 1840–1890*, edited and compiled by Kenneth L. Holmes. Vol. 1. Glendale, Calif.: The Arthur H. Clark Company, 1983.

National Geographic Society, Special Publications Division. *Trails West*. Washington, D.C.: National Geographic Society, 1979.

Watkins, T. H. *Gold and Silver in the West/An Illustrated History of an American Dream*. Palo Alto, Calif.: American West Publishing Company, 1971.

Mary Ellen Todd:

Clayman, Charles B., ed. *The American Medical Association Encyclopedia of Medicine*. New York: Random House, 1989.

Hixon, Adrietta Applegate. *On to Oregon! A True Story of a Young Girl's Journey Into the West*. Weiser, Idaho: Signal-American Printers, 1947.

Moser, Don. *The Snake River Country*. The American Wilderness Series. Alexandria, Va.: Time-Life Books, 1977.

Lucy Ann Henderson:

Commager, Henry Steele. *The West: An Illustrated History*. Edited by Marcus Cunliffe and Maldwyn A. Jones. New York: Promontory Press, 1976.

Davidson, James West and Mark H. Lytle. *The United States: A History of the Republic*, 249–256. Englewood Cliffs, N.J.: Prentice-Hall, Inc., 1981.

Deady, Mrs. Matthew P. "Crossing the Plains to Oregon in 1846." Interview by Fred Lockley. *Transactions of the Oregon Pioneer Association* (1928): 57-64.

Thornton, J. Quinn. *The Far Western Frontier: Oregon and California in 1848.* Vols. 1 and 2. New York: Harper & Brothers, 1849. Reprint, New York: Arno Press, 1973.

Laura Ingalls:

Anderson, William. *Laura Ingalls Wilder: A Biography.* New York: HarperCollins Publishers, Inc., 1992.

Wilder, Laura Ingalls. Illustrated by Garth Williams. Autobiographical series of "Little House" books: *Little House in the Big Woods, Little House on the Prairie, Farmer Boy, On the Banks of Plum Creek, By the Shores of Silver Lake, The Long Winter, Little Town on the Prairie, These Happy Golden Years, The First Four Years.* New York, Evanston, San Francisco, and London: Harper & Row, 1971.

Wilder, Laura Ingalls. *On the Way Home: The Diary of a Trip from South Dakota to Mansfield, Missouri, in 1894.* New York and Evanston Ill.: Harper & Row, 1962.

Wilder, Laura Ingalls. *West From Home/Letters of Laura Ingalls Wilder, San Francisco, 1915.* Edited by Roger Lea MacBride. New York: Harper & Row, 1974.

Zochert, Donald. *Laura: The Life of Laura Ingalls Wilder.* New York: Avon Books, 1977.

Mary Perry:

Frost, Mary Perry. "Experience of a Pioneer." *The Washington Quarterly,* (Washington University State Historical Society) vol. 7, no. 2 (1916): 123–125.

Frost, Mary Perry. Untitled interview published in the *Tacoma Sunday Ledger,* 26 June 1892.

Frost, Mary Perry. "Pays Tribute to Mother." *Tacoma News,* 15 April 1915.

Schlissel, Lillian. *Women's Diaries of the Westward Journey.* New York: Schocken Books, 1982.

Catherine Sager:

Jeffrey, Julie Roy. *Converting the West: A Biography of Narcissa Whitman.* Norman, Okla., and London: University of Oklahoma Press, 1991.

Lockley, Fred. *Conversations with Pioneer Women.* Compiled and edited by Mike Helm. Eugene, Ore.: Rainy Day Press, 1981.

Pringle, Catherine Sager. Journal as copied from the original manuscript by Edmond S. Meany for the University of Washington, Seattle, 1908. Catherine Sager's journal (FAC 600) is quoted by permission of The Huntington Library, San Marino, Calif.

Sager, Catherine, Elizabeth, and Matilda. *The Whitman Massacre of 1847.* Fairfield, Wash.: Ye Galleon Press, 1981.

Thompson, Erwin N. *Shallow Grave at Waiilatpu: The Sagers' West.* Western Imprints, the Press of the Oregon Historical Society. Second edition, revised. Third Printing, 1985.

Martha Ann Morrison:

Lowe, Beverly Elizabeth. *John Minto: Man of Courage 1822–1915.* Salem, Ore.: Kingston Price and Company, 1980.

Minto, Mrs. M. A. "Female Pioneering in Oregon." Dictation of Martha Ann Morrison Minto taken by H. H. Bancroft, 1878. Quoted by permission of the Bancroft Library, University of California, Berkeley, from the original manuscript (P-A 51).

Susan Thompson and Olive Oatman:

Faulk, Odie B. *Destiny Road: The Gila Trail and the Opening of the Southwest.* New York: Oxford University Press, 1973.

National Geographic Society, Special Publications Division. *Trails West.* Washington, D.C.: National Geographic Society, 1979.

Oatman, Olive. Personal narrative. Center for Archival Collections, Jerome Library, Bowling Green State University, Bowling Green, Ohio.

Parrish, Susan Thompson Lewis. Transcripts of "Following the Pot of Gold at the Rainbow's End in the Days of 1850." The Huntington Library Collection, San Marino, Calif.

Stratton, R.B. *Captivity of the Oatman Girls.* Upper Saddle River, N.J.: Literature House, an imprint of The Gregg Press, 1970.

Maps:

Western Emigrant Trails 1830–1870: Major Trails, Cutoffs, and Alternates, second edition, 1991, 1993. Published by the Oregon-California Trails Association. Robert L. Berry, Map Project Editor. James A. Bier, Cartographer.

National Geographic Society, Special Publications Division. *Trails West.* Washington, D.C., National Geographic Society, 1979. (Maps of the Gila, Santa Fe, California, and Oregon Trails.)

INDEX

A

American Lake 55
Apache Indians 76, 77, 78, 81
Applegate, Jesse 35
Applegate, John 30
Applegate, Mary Ellen Todd
    21–22, 24–31
Applegate Trail 35
Arkansas River 76

B

Barlow Road 29
Bloomington, Indiana 13
Blue Mountains 28, 61
Breen, Margaret 7, 8
Breen, Patrick 7, 8
bridge *23*
Burr Oak, Iowa 46

C

cannibalism, of Donner party 8
Cascade Mountains 29–30, 53
Cayuse Indians 62, 63–64

cholera 15, 21–22, 24
Clatsop Plains 71–72
Columbia River 28, 29, 64, 71
Continental Divide 2, 16
Cronin, John 55

D

Dagon, Theophilos 58, 60, 61, 62
Dalles, The 71
Deady, Edward 39
Deady, Henderson B. 39
Deady, Lucy Ann Henderson
    33–35, 37–39
Deady, Mary 39
Deady, Matthew P. 38–39
Deady, Paul 39
De Smet, South Dakota 47–49
Devil's Gate 16, *17*
diphtheria 48–49
Donner, George 2
Donner, Mary 10
Donner Lake 6, 9–10
Donner party 1–11, 19

E

Eliza 2
Eureka, Nevada 20

F

Fort Boise 28
Fort Bridger 2, 69
Fort Hall 27, 35, 60
Fort Kearney 15
Fort Laramie 15, 27, 35, 58
Fort Vancouver 64, 71
Fort Walla Walla 64
Forty Mile Desert 16, 18
Fort Yuma 78, 80, 83
Francisco 83
Fremont, California 19
Frost, Andrew J. 55–56
Frost, Mary Perry 51–53, 55–56
Frost, Walter G. 56

G

Gates Post Office, Nebraska *54*
Gila Trail 78, 80
gold rush, California 10, 14
Grant family 26–27
Great Salt Lake 2, 4
Green River 27, 60

H

Hastings, Lansford W. 2
Henderson, Lettie 33–34, 37, 39
Henderson, Lucy Ann 33–35, 37–39
Henderson, Olivia 37, 39
Henderson, Rhoda 33–35, 37–38
Henderson, Robert 33–35, 37–38
Hester, Craven P. 14, 19, 20
Hester, John 14, 16

Hester, Lottie 14, 15 , 16
Hester, Martha 14, 15, 19
Hester, Sallie 13–20
Hester, William 14
Hixon, Adrietta Applegate 21
Howell's Prairie 30
Hudson's Bay Company 51, 64
Humboldt River 5, 16, 35

I

Independence, Missouri 2, 24, 75
Independence Rock 15
Ingalls, Caroline 41–48, 49
Ingalls, Carrie 41, *43,* 44–46, 48, 49
Ingalls, Charles 41–48, 49
Ingalls, Eliza A. 45, 46
Ingalls, Freddie 41, 46
Ingalls, Grace 41, 46, 49
Ingalls, Laura Elizabeth 41–50, *43*
Ingalls, Mary 42, *43,* 44–47
Ingalls, Peter 45, 46

K

Kaw River 25

L

Lafayette, Oregon 38
Lassen Meadows 35
laudanum 33
Laura Ingalls Wilder Home and Museum 50
Laurel Hill 29–30
Lewis, David 83
Lewis, Susan Thompson 75–78, 80–81, 83–84
Little House in the Big Woods 42

M

Maddock, James K. 20
Maddock, Sallie Hester 13–20
malaria 44
Mansfield, Missouri 49–50
measles 63
Minto, John 67–73, *70*
Minto, John W. *70*, 73
Minto, Mary Ellen 73
Missouri River 13, 57
Mohave Indians 81–83
Morrison, Hanna 68
Morrison, James F. 68
Morrison, John 68
Morrison, Martha Ann 67–73, *70*
Morrison, Mary Ann 68
Morrison, Nancy 68, 71–72
Morrison, Thomas 68
Morrison, Wilson 68, 69, 71–72
mountain fever 27, 28
Murphy, John 10
Murphy, Virginia Reed 1–11, *3*

N

Natchez Pass 53
Natchez River 53
Native Americans 12, 26, 52. *See
    also under* specific tribe

O

Oatman, Lorenzo 79, 83
Oatman, Lucy 75–79
Oatman, Mary Ann 79, 81
Oatman, Mrs. 79
Oatman, Olive 75–79, 81–84, *82*
Oatman, Royce 76, 78–79
Oatman Flat 84
Ogden, Peter Skene 64

Ohio River 13
Oregon–California Trail 34
Oregon City, Oregon 38, 64
Osage Indians 44

P

Pepin, Wisconsin 42
Perry, Mary 51–53, 55–56
Perry, Mrs. 51, 53–55
Perry, Walter 51, 53
Pima Indians 78
pioneer palace car 1–2
Platte River 2, 15, 22, 24, 35, 57
Plum Creek 45
Polk, James K. 34
Portland, Oregon 39
Pringle, Catherine Sager 57–66, *59*
Pringle, Clark S. 65

Q

Quiner, Henry 42, 44
Quiner, Polly 42, 44

R

Ragsdale, John 24, 29
Reed, James 2, 4, 7, 9
Reed, James F. 1, 4, 5, 9–10
Reed, Margaret 2, 7, 9, 10, 20
Reed, Patty 2, 4, 7, 9–10, 11
Reed, Thomas 2, 4, 7, 9–10
Reed, Virginia 1–11, *3*
Rio Grande River 77
Roberts, Rev. William M. 65
Rocky Mountain spotted fever 27
Rocky Ridge Farm 49–50

S

Sager, Catherine 57–66, *59*

Sager, Elizabeth M. 57–58, 64–65
Sager, Francis 58, 63, 64
Sager, Hannah Louise 57–58, 61, 64
Sager, Henrietta Naomi 62, 63, 64–65
Sager, Henry 57–58, 60, 67–68
Sager, John 58, 63, 64
Sager, Matilda J. 57–58, 62–63, 64–65
Sager, Naomi 57–58, 60–61, 67
Sager, Rosanna 58, 60–61
Salem, Oregon 65, 72, 73
San Gabriel River 80–81
San Jose, California 20
Santa Fe Trail 76
Shaw, Mrs. 61
Shaw, William 57, 60–62
Shoshone Indians 27
Sierra Nevada Mountains 1, 5–11, 18–19
Silver Lake, South Dakota 47–49
Sleepy Hollow 19
Snake River 27, 30
Sonoran Desert 78
South Pass 16
Spokane, Washington 66
Springfield, Illinois 1
St. Joseph, Missouri 13, 14
Sutter's Fort 4, 5, 6, 10
Sweetwater River 16, 27

T

Thompson, Gila 80
Thompson, Mr. 80
Thompson, Mrs. 80
Thompson, Susan 75–78, 80–81, 83–84
Thornton, J. Quinn 35

Todd, Abbot 21–22, 24–30
Todd, Angelina 21–22, 24–30
Todd, Cynthia 22, 24, 25, 28, 30
Todd, Elijah 28
Todd, Louvina 21–22, 25, 30
Todd, Mary Ellen 21–22, 24–31
Truckee River 18
Tucson, Arizona 77–78
typhoid fever 60, 67–68

W

wagon, interior of *36*
Waiilatpu, Washington 61
Walnut Grove, Minnesota 45, 46–47
Whitman, Marcus 61–64
Whitman, Narcissa 61–64
Whitman Mission 61–64
Wilder, Almanzo 41, 48–50
Wilder, Laura Elizabeth Ingalls 41–50, *43*
Wilder, Rose 48–49
Willamette Valley 37, 38

Z

Zumbro River 45

⅂|⅃9 5

ABOUT THE AUTHOR

Mary Barmeyer O'Brien was born and raised in Missoula, Montana, and received a B.A. from Linfield College in McMinnville, Oregon. She is also the author of *Heart of the Trail* and *Jeannette Rankin: Bright Star in the Big Sky*, a biography for young readers. Her magazine articles for both children and adults have appeared in many national publications including *Northwest Living!, Ladies' Home Journal, Jack and Jill, Catholic Parent, Living with Preschoolers,* and *Glacier Valley.* Mary works from her home in Polson, Montana, where she lives with her husband, Dan, who is a high school biology teacher, and their three children, Jennifer, Kevin, and Katie.